Leading and coaching teams to success

"Coaching remains an underused leadership style. This book offers a usable, practice-led guide to developing the skills to broaden your leadership repertoire. Phil draws on his years of experience as both a leader and a coach to provide insight into coaching successfully, not just with individuals but also with teams. A welcome addition to the expanding coaching canon."

Andy Firth, Senior Consultant, Roffey Park Institute, UK

Leading and coaching teams to success

The secret life of teams

Philip Hayes

Open University Press
McGraw-Hill Education
McGraw-Hill House
Shoppenhangers Road
Maidenhead
Berkshire
England
SL6 2QL

email: enquiries@openup.co.uk
world wide web: www.openup.co.uk

and Two Penn Plaza, New York, NY 10121-2289, USA

First published 2011

A catalogue record of this book is available from the British Library

ISBN-13: 978-0-33-523852-1 (pb) 978-0-33-523853-8 (hb)
ISBN-10: 0-33-523852-1 (pb) 0-33-523853-X (hb)
eISBN: 978-0-33-523854-5

Library of Congress Cataloging-in-Publication Data
CIP data applied for

Typesetting and e-book compilations by
RefineCatch Limited, Bungay, Suffolk
Printed in the UK by Bell & Bain Ltd, Glasgow

Fictitious names of companies, products, people, characters and/or data that may be used herein (in case studies or in examples) are not intended to represent any real individual, company, product or event.

The *McGraw·Hill* Companies

Contents

Preface

I loved being in teams when I was a kid in Glasgow; being lined up against the playground wall and picked for ad hoc soccer games. For me the best part of scouting was venturing out as a team to sea or on mountain expeditions. I loved playing cricket, hockey and rugby for my secondary school and singing in a festival-winning choir. I even loved being in a platoon in the army cadet force, despite horrible scratchy uniforms.

I valued the moments of achievement, the camaraderie and the sense of belonging. I can remember with absolute clarity the delicious pleasure of seeing my name on the team sheet on the school notice board, or walking with my choir onto the podium to perform at the Blackpool Winter Gardens knowing we were strong contenders to win. My own home was not a particularly nurturing place, so teams became alternative homes, providing friendship and security, where I could compete with others and advance on my own merit. There were clear rules, a pecking order and opportunities to gain kudos. It was important to me that these team activities were run largely on a fair, equal and transparent basis.

The pleasure and pride associated with being in teams seemed to weaken disappointingly as adult life arrived. At university I discovered that, beyond school, team participation was an irregular, even dissipated phenomenon. Partly this was because no one actually *had* to join – it was all voluntary – and this made it hard to work out the worth of any given team. Rules were looser, points of entry, no longer governed by age group, more various and behavioural norms harder to establish. It also became harder to know if the team was succeeding or not, and I liked to be in winning teams.

The work environment was even more disappointing. The first work 'teams' I joined lacked common purpose and were full of individuals intent on enhancing their personal status. I made a move to working in social services, where I experienced small 'shift' based teams that were somewhat more cohesive but still failed to offer the purposeful, competitive camaraderie I had thrived on when younger.

Then something changed. I remember vividly my first ever encounter with management theory relating to the leadership of teams. I was a London-based local authority social worker receiving my first ever formal training in leadership – a half day seminar, which was considered sufficient at the time for someone leading a team of about fourteen other social workers. The trainer was a sardonic American whose delivery conveyed weary disdain both for his material and for his audience. Nevertheless, it turned out to be a revelatory experience for me. Drawing on the flipchart a Venn diagram of three intersecting circles labelled 'Task', 'Team' and 'Individual', the trainer explained that leaders of teams needed to pay attention to each of these three domains if they were to achieve sustainable performance. This led to an analysis of behaviours needed for effective leadership. It was my introduction to the work of John Adair and his stalwart 'Action Centred Leadership' model (Adair, 1973).

I had begun the seminar with no idea that there was anything more to leading teams than a democratic instinct, a sense of fairness and a willingness to set an example by doing well in my own job. I had encountered a smattering of psychological and sociological theory, but it had not occurred to me that such thinking could be applied to the problems of leadership.

The seminar had a powerful influence on me. On a practical level, I resolved to become a much better team leader. I also discovered an interest in the theory of leadership. And it occurred to me that I could make a better fist of delivering the training than the sardonic American – a thought that was to gain fuller expression a few years later when I made the transition to leadership training and development as a career.

What remains from that seminar is the conviction that the right knowledge and skill can be crucial in enabling a leader to develop a team and lead it to success. That belief has led, thirty years on, to the writing of this book.

Continuing to practise as a social worker, I widened my reading. I encountered a variety of sociological theories, explored systems theory, particularly in relation to families, and I studied the psychodynamic model of counselling. It was in the psychodynamics of individuals and groups that I seemed to find the secret of how teams worked – or, more often, failed to work. The subtitle of this book, 'The Secret Life of Teams', springs largely from my vivid personal experience of being a member of a series of 'process' groups. Some of these encounters, in retrospect, echoed the pioneering work of Wilfred Bion, who described the reactions of participants in groups that had been set up with no agenda or purpose other than the examination of group dynamics (Bion, 1968). My first experience of such a group followed a predictable pattern. Our behaviours ranged from curious to furious as we strove to make sense of what was happening to us. Most of us wanted a task to work on or agenda to follow and were mystified and frustrated when the facilitator merely reflected back to us what she perceived us to be doing and saying. The emotional aspects of our interaction seemed to take on a heightened and almost unreal quality as we struggled to understand the intellectual premise – that we were experiencing what happens to us as individuals and as a group when there is no other agenda than this process of examination – and to accept that there was nothing to focus on except the raw dynamics themselves.

The idea that the group was a laboratory of pure process took a while to sink in. For me, when the penny eventually dropped, it was like looking at one of those 'magic eye' pictures where one's focus suddenly shifts to reveal a completely new landscape. Although I had understood intellectually that much of our behaviour is rooted in unconscious drivers created in the crucible of our earliest relationships, the recognition of the power of these unconscious forces was emotionally intoxicating.

Some of the learning from subsequent groups was uncomfortable as I recognised primitive root motivations behind my behaviours. In fact so unsettling were some of the revelations about my deeper self that I signed up for a couple of years of personal therapy for good measure.

The last group of this sort I participated in – part of a Master's degree programme in Management Learning – gave me a fresh perspective.

The tension and frustration I was experiencing from sitting in an apparently endless session was becoming too much for me to handle. I stood up, announced I was going into another room to think about my current essay assignment, and invited anyone who felt so inclined to join me for an academic discussion. This struck me as an act of rebellion, even heresy – no one had left the group before and it felt taboo to do so. When I entered the other room and turned round I was astounded at the number who had followed me. It seemed everyone wanted to get out of the vortex and channel their energies into something with overt purpose. This was a first practical realisation of the power of active purpose in groups – and a personal lesson in leadership.

Meanwhile, my narrow focus on unconscious dynamics was being challenged by new learning. Neuro-Linguistic Programming (NLP) became a particular interest. I explored experiential learning, Transactional Analysis and Gestalt. The emergence in management development circles of influential new waves of writers on organisational theory and on ecological and systemic approaches enriched my understanding of team development.

My sense that the team lived in a goldfish-bowl of unconscious intra-and-inter-personal dynamics became overlaid with a more complex understanding of the cultural and organisational forces to which the team is inevitably subject. Having focused so intently on the process of helping teams manage their dynamics, I became increasingly interested in working with them pragmatically to achieve effective outcomes.

This has been quite a journey. I have had to learn to shift my ego out of the way and to value the ongoing progress of the team above the process of the training, however insightful. I have reached a point now where I know I can never hope to know it all, but I know at least some of what I don't know.

Introduction

This book is for you if you are a practising team coach or aspire to be one, whether you operate inside an organisation or independently; if you are a facilitator, HR professional, trainer or consultant who wants to learn more about team development and grow your repertoire of skills; if you are the leader or manager of a team and want to be as effective as possible in that role; or if you simply want to understand more about how teams work.

I have written it firmly from a practitioner's perspective – it is based on over twenty years experience of developing teams as a trainer, consultant and coach in a wide range of organisations – and I often speak directly to the reader who is working in a coaching role. At the same time, I write with an awareness of the wider challenges of team membership, and the value to the team leader of knowledge and skills usually associated more with coaching than with managing.

A team coach, as distinct from a trainer or consultant, works to help a team learn and improve performance over a period of time rather than as a one-off intervention; helps the team to be conscious of its own interactions and processes and to learn from them; and uses facilitation and coaching skills to help a team have skilful and effective discussions.

It is a demanding role covering a wide set of skills and qualities, including the need to exercise shrewd interpersonal and political intelligence. It makes huge demands on the coach's ability to self manage. It can be stressful. But it is also a fascinating and rewarding role because teams can learn so quickly and can make astounding leaps forward in performance.

The secret life of teams

The reality of working with teams rarely reflects the analytical detachment of many management texts. It is an intense experience involving very real flesh and blood people, and can sometimes feel rather like being in a soap opera. Teams are made up of all kinds of people and it is what goes on inside them as individuals and between them as a group that is often at the heart of what the team coach has to deal with. Each team, even if engineered to an organisational blueprint and designed to represent the prevailing culture, will be unique, often bafflingly so, in its complex human interactions and dynamics. Understanding the balance of interpersonal team dynamics with cultural and systemic factors in deciding where to put your skills and effort is one of the fascinating and demanding tasks that fall to the team coach.

Some aspects of team interaction might not seem secret at all. Much discussion and conversation within teams is public, in the sense that it is conducted in meetings, in open plan offices and in a variety of open settings, both formal and informal. A team coach will spend a high proportion of his or her time managing carefully constructed meetings in which conversation is at its most public and, to some degree, managed or staged. So what *is* 'secret' about team life? Here are some of the secret dimensions:

- Many team conversations happen when not all of the team is present, amongst friendship groups or alliances, and what is said in this more selective context can be very different from what is said in the context of the whole team.
- 'Off-line' conversations over coffee or in the bar can show up real discrepancies between what people say in public and what they really think and feel and are prepared to divulge only to their confidants.
- The body language of participants in team meetings and events can reveal a discrepancy between the words they speak and their private thoughts and feelings.

An important part of the coach's job is to bring these unmentioned issues into the conversation.

The elephant in the room

It is a well-known phenomenon in teams – the issue that is commonly known about (although frequently not by everyone), routinely discussed in private by sub-groups, but never referred to within the team as a whole at official team meetings. At one level it is as if the issue does not exist, but at another level it preoccupies much of the conscious and unconscious energy of the team. 'Elephants' I have come across frequently include:

- The feeling that the team is failing and indeed cannot succeed in its task
- Serious doubts about the competency or credibility of the team leader or other team member
- Rivalry or enmity between group members
- Issues of poor performance
- Poor personal or interpersonal behaviour
- Scandal of some sort involving one or more team members
- Unacknowledged competition for power, for promotion or for a specific role in the team

- Issues of status, e.g. some roles being considered more important than others
- Feelings of being bullied, overlooked or otherwise disrespected on the part of one or more members of the team
- Issues around fairness
- Favouritism on the part of the leader

These elephants can be corrosive and demoralising in their effect. One of the main practical benefits a team coach can bring to the party is to publicly 'name' the elephant in an impartial and non-prejudicial way. *Naming* of issues is usually the first step in identifying them as legitimate and necessary subjects of discussion, and the first step to *taming* them – putting them in perspective, examining their causes and resolving to deal with them. This is sensitive work; the naming of a taboo issue can sometimes feel risky for the team coach. It is an area in which offering the team an exercise of some sort can be a useful way of highlighting a topic that is hard to discuss: often behaviours that happen during these exercises are a direct analogue to what happens when the team is engaged in its real work.

People rarely if ever speak the 'whole truth and nothing but the truth' in business conversations – we all tend to hold back something, be it a personal opinion, an anxiety or something we simply don't want others to know. I believe from long experience of coaching and being coached that even in the so-called 'safe' context of one-to-one coaching there are areas we all choose to keep to ourselves. This is perhaps a surprising proposition bearing in mind these are private conversations conducted under strict rules of confidentiality and between people whose level of mutual trust is usually high, but I have yet to find a colleague who disagrees with me on this. And disclosure during team coaching involves more risk.

Organisations are intrinsically political, and inevitably this is reflected in the life of teams. Sometimes 'politicking' is more or less overt and seen as part of the accepted currency of organisational and team life. In other contexts, behaving openly in a 'political' way can be frowned on. For example, in some charities and public service organisations there can be an espoused culture of dedicated, selfless idealism in which, at its most extreme, pursuit of personal interest is seen as unworthy. But I have yet to experience any team in which there is no political agenda whatsoever. If pressed I would assert that often the teams in which political behaviour is openly acknowledged have a healthier psychological climate than those in which all energy and behaviour is supposed to be channelled towards selfless endeavour. To put it simply, the more 'do-goody' an organisation is the more it seems to struggle with managing its competitive instincts.

The tension between collaborative behaviour and individual competitiveness is one of the fascinating dimensions of team life and it takes many forms.

The team coach can never hope to know all the secrets of the team. The skill is to understand that underneath the public arena of each team there is *always* a complex set of competing, often hidden agendas and driving forces, both personal and interpersonal. It is vital to be able to spot at least the major signs and symptoms of these, and to judge when and how to take these into account when working with the team.

Most of us would recognise these as the informal undercurrents of team life. But what of the deeper secrets that might be less commonly understood?

The unconscious dimension of team life

At the heart of all group interaction is a set of primal unconscious individual preoccupations with issues such as psychological safety, acceptance and intimacy. Wilfred Bion wrote about what he called the Basic Assumption (BA) group, whose underlying preoccupations were with what he described as dependency, 'flight/fight' and pairing issues (Bion, 1968). This 'BA' group dynamic would coexist with what he termed the Work Group dynamic, that collective group energy which goes towards collective effort and task achievement. When something threatening occurs to the group dynamic causing anxiety, the BA dynamic asserts itself, manifesting itself in behaviours such as infighting or passivity. The group gets caught up in an unconscious collusion to protect itself.

The team coach can learn to spot the signs of unconscious preoccupations that may be creating group anxiety and task dysfunction by paying attention to the nuances of group communication, both verbal and non-verbal. I have noticed, for example, that groups who persistently complain about temperature, lighting, quality of refreshments or room comfort are often engaging with an unconscious preoccupation about how they are being treated by the wider organisation, and whether or not they feel safe. Listening with a third ear to some of these unconscious themes can be extremely illuminating.

To be a team coach is not to be a therapist and it is not the role of the generalist team coach to delve deeply into the unconscious roots of specific interpersonal dynamics; apart from anything else there is usually too much else to do. But these roots are a persistent undercurrent to all the team's interpersonal behaviours. A working knowledge of core psychodynamic theories and processes can help the team coach to understand something of why certain behaviours in teams can seem mystifying. I once worked with a team in which a powerful middle-aged female executive behaved confidently and assertively with all her colleagues except one. He was a slightly older man who carried himself with a quiet authority. When she spoke to him her body language and tone of voice would change quite dramatically and become almost girlish. She seemed unable to assert herself. I later had the opportunity to coach the woman individually and the topic of her relationship with this man came up.

She was at a loss to know why she found him intimidating. We did an exercise called the meta-mirror, a Gestalt-derived exercise which enables someone to look at a relationship from different perceptual positions. From this more detached perspective she was able to see that when she was in the presence of this man she felt as she had felt as a young girl sitting with her father. There was something about the way she saw this colleague that connected her with these powerful early feelings and it was from these feelings that she would behave when in his presence. With this revelation she was able to marshal her personal resourcefulness, revert to adult mode and effect a radical change in her relationship with the man.

The art of coaching

Leading and coaching teams is not a science. I recently had the pleasure and challenge of helping to crew a large nineteenth-century sailing ship and learned a lot from observing the captain's behaviour, and talking with him about the task of running the ship. When embarking on a voyage as captain, you will set course with clear conviction as to your destination; you will know everything there is to know about how to work the ship mechanically; you will understand the techniques of navigation. But still the weather can change surprisingly, some of the passengers or even crew may behave in unpredictable ways, and there may even be structural or mechanical problems with the ship you were previously unaware of. You may need to change course, even change your destination. Sometimes you may need to be very actively involved, leading at first hand and by example: sometimes you need to leave the crew to get on with it.

Like captaining a ship, team leadership and coaching is an art requiring full attention, an active intelligence directed at subtle nuances of behaviour and mood, and an almost endless series of fine judgement calls in the midst of swirling vortices of change. It can be exhilarating and satisfying: and occasionally, when the storms roll in, it can be a waking nightmare.

Leadership and coaching

There is a growing acceptance that leaders can usefully coach individual staff. There is as yet less emphasis on the value of leaders coaching their teams. The leader is called upon to lead in a number of different ways according to circumstance, but can certainly use a coaching approach when helping the team to learn and improve its processes of working. Being part of the team – and an extremely important part – the leader cannot have the detached perspective of the external coach, but can at times play an equivalent role to great effect. See Chapter 3 for more on this.

The changing face of teams

A lot has changed in organisational life since I entered the world of work in the 1970s. Performance demands have risen sharply in both public and private sectors. Teams are changing rapidly in the way they are put together and asked to work: the team is now the paramount model and means for achieving organisational performance. Senior directors increasingly work in multi-disciplinary, strategic leadership teams – a far cry from the traditional specialist 'silo' approach where there was little emphasis on working collaboratively. In addition there is a sharp increase in the use of ad hoc or short-term project teams that operate at many levels within organisations. These need to acquire a strong shared working ethos and to develop their performance capability quickly.

To add to the demands placed on the modern flexible team we are now seeing in the UK the rise of partnership teams working between separate organisations (for example, between teams composed of staff from local government and the health service). These partnership arrangements, made to facilitate more 'joined up' management of service delivery, are dependent on teams from two or more organisations working together. The challenge of building effective teams from different organisational cultures is often daunting. Even more daunting is the fact that, in a global economy populated by multi-national companies, many teams operate in different time-zones, are composed of disparate cultures and speak different languages – the virtual team is with us.

A lot rests on how all these different kinds of teams perform – not least for the reputations of those who lead them and work in them. Pressure on team performance in recent times has been pumped up still further by the current economic crisis and by the enormous governmental and media pressure applied to organisations to achieve and deliver. Teams of all sorts need to be able to learn and perform simultaneously – and they need to reach full effectiveness extremely quickly. There has never been a more compelling context for investing in the development of teams.

Hence the rising interest in how to lead and coach teams effectively – and the emergence of the new breed of specialist team coach. In addition there is increasing emphasis on leaders and managers as coaches, both of individual staff and of their teams. There is as yet little consistency of view on how leaders or managers should do this, and throughout the book you will read ideas from different sources for leaders of teams who wish to take an effective coaching approach.

Practical emphasis

This book will have a strong emphasis on practical ideas, techniques and skills for getting the best out of a team in a variety of contexts. These have been thoroughly road-tested by me or by trusted colleagues – or at least are drawn from close observation, such as from watching a variety of leaders perform. Some ideas will be useful for those of you who are making your way in organisational life and want to make the most of membership of your current team. Other ideas will be useful specifically for leaders, still others for those who are professionally concerned with team development as a part of your role, for example in Human Resources or Organisational Development. Though some techniques and exercises are described in a specific context, most can be used flexibly across a wide range of situations.

I absolutely do not claim to know it all and am resigned to never doing so, but hope that I can offer some ideas and concepts that you will find useful in your own work. I am not offering a proprietary brand of team coaching but an integrative approach based on extensive practical experience.

The role of theory

The field of theory relating to teams is broad, drawing on aspects of psychology, sociology, organisational theory and systems theory among others. Some of the theories may appear contradictory or paradoxical and, for this reason alone, theory has to remain as a background influence rather than as an ideological or methodological driver. Where I introduce or describe a particular theory, it is always with the underlying assumption that the theory may interest you and inform your thinking, understanding and action, but will not be a prescription or an instruction.

You can never apply a theory in any direct way, but understanding at least some of the major theories relating to teams is an essential part of your armoury as a team coach or leader. This is not least because many members of teams are quite knowledgeable about leadership and management theory themselves and may test your knowledge – and thus your credibility. More positively, theory can provide useful reference points, helping you and your team to identify where they might be in their development – or why they are experiencing frustration or blockage. Finally, theoretical models can provide insight for teams, offering new understanding and with it potential for learning and development. This is particularly true for those team members who have a theoretical learning style preference.

One of the factors that makes team coaching powerful is the potential it holds for collective and individual learning: if individuals are able to learn from their interaction with each other it is likely to be a very powerful form of personal learning, especially given the primary role group life has in shaping our sense of personal identity and social belonging.

Case studies

Throughout this book, the practice of team leadership and coaching will be illustrated by reference to examples drawn from actual experience. Naturally the identity of specific teams and individuals will remain anonymous, using alternative names where appropriate. In some cases, where certain syndromes recur, aspects of different stories will be conflated. They will still be essentially true stories – or as true as one person's perspective on them allows them to be.

Summary of chapters

Chapter 1 – How to be a successful team member

- The importance of being an effective team member
- How to create the right impact and make joining a team successful
- Managing relationships and being appropriately assertive
- Influencing effectively in a team context
- Ensuring you are clear about what is expected of you
- Fitting in well and playing to your strengths
- Getting the support you need and managing your development
- Becoming a valued colleague and offering support to your team mates
- Strategies for dealing effectively with conflict
- Making the right impact at meetings
- Managing your time and workload
- Managing your boss

Chapter 2 – Essential skills for team leaders and coaches

- Understanding the role of the team coach
- The personal qualities needed to be an effective team coach
- Essential skills: learning about the team, contracting, creating rapport and asking powerful questions
- Skills and knowledge drawn from executive coaching
- Skills and knowledge drawn from facilitation practice
- Skills and knowledge drawn from team building practice
- Skills and knowledge drawn from process consulting

Chapter 3 – The coaching approach to leading teams

- What a coaching approach can offer the team leader
- How leaders can use coaching skills in practice
- The critical importance of trust for the team leader
- The need for the leader to believe in the team
- When *not* to use a coaching style as a team leader
- The climate model of leadership – a framework for success
- Key personal leadership behaviours that produce high performance in teams

Chapter 4 – The challenge of the high performing team

- The particular challenge involved in coaching successful teams
- Leadership and *vision*
- Leadership and *trust*
- Making the most of a variety of talents and abilities
- Creating targets for success
- Running effective team meetings
- Sustaining high performance and keeping it focused on organisational need

Chapter 5 – Handling the problematic team

- Goal setting with problematic teams
- Working with macho teams
- Six challenging teams: case studies
- Toxic teams and what causes them
- Handling difficult behaviours
- Taking care of yourself

Chapter 6 – Designing interventions

- Design principles and the importance of flexibility
- Understanding learning styles
- Games and simulations: their merits and dangers
- Icebreakers and introductory exercises
- Models and processes to help teams think and learn
- Review techniques
- Agenda building as a team activity
- Managing feedback

Chapter 7 – The impact of organisational culture

- Cultural and systemic influences on teams
- Understanding organisational culture
- Team exercises that explore organisational structure
- The importance of language and metaphor in understanding team cultures
- Teams that organisational culture forgot: case studies

Chapter 8 – Further resources for team leaders and coaches

- A selection of useful contact details and websites
- Guidance for using outdoor team development organisations
- A selection of games and simulations with review notes
- The team coach's tool kit

Each chapter ends with a summary of *key learning points* and a short selection of *reflective questions* for the reader.

1 How to be a successful team member

With so much emphasis in management literature placed on the leadership role, it is easy to overlook the importance of the team members, whose individual performances can be crucial to overall success. Even when you lead a team, it is highly likely that you will continue to participate as a member of other teams. Being seen as an effective team player can have a significant impact on your career development. This involves understanding yourself, understanding other people and managing your relationships over months or years.

Team membership can be a delight and a source of strength, learning, comradeship and support. Being part of a successfully functioning team can be wonderfully fulfilling. Being part of a dysfunctional and failing team can be challenging, even miserable. Yet very little is written about this important subject: it seems we are expected to find our own way over the social, emotional, psychological and behavioural hurdles that team membership can at times present.

Joining a team

Team membership begins in childhood. Our early experiences are extremely important in shaping our attitudes to teams and our thoughts and feelings about participating in them. For most of us our first 'team' was our family, and there can be no doubt that factors such as birth order, sibling relationships, the family roles we were cast in and the way we were treated by our parents or carers leaves us with a deep legacy of responses, conscious and unconscious, to group situations. Then school introduces us to new kinds of teams – friendship groups, sports teams, clubs and societies.

As a child in the 1960s I attended a tough Glaswegian primary school opposite Ibrox Stadium, home to the powerful Glasgow Rangers. For the boys, football was unchallenged as the only important game and was played every day before school began, in every break, and for long sessions after school.

Huge kudos was attached to prowess at the game – kudos that could be achieved otherwise only through fighting ability or being exceptionally clever in class. Every match would start with a ritual for picking the teams. The two best players would toss a coin for first pick, whilst the rest of us lined up against the wall. The captains would then choose in turn. I remember how my heart would leap if I were picked early, and how it would sink if I came lower down the order. Being picked early was even more important than playing for the better team. Prestige and a sense of inclusion were at stake.

At school age we are strongly affected by our concerns about team issues such as:

- Will I be safe?
- Will I be chosen?
- Will I fit in?
- Will I have friends or allies?
- Where will I be in the pecking order?
- What will be expected of me?

We probably experienced these not as fully-formed conscious thoughts but as feelings of anxiety, the strength of feeling depending on a wide range of factors both psychological and situational.

It is important for each of us to understand something of how our attitude to early-life team membership continues to influence our feelings and behaviour as adults. When we come to join teams in adult life we will certainly revisit at least some of the feelings we had in childhood. The nature and strength of these feelings will vary widely from person to person.

Most of us manage our feelings about being in teams more effectively as we progress through our careers and as the process of joining and participating in teams becomes more familiar. However, we will still be powerfully affected by assumptions about ourselves in relation to teams that stem from fundamental influences. Our ability to cope well with the issues attached to joining a team will depend significantly upon the degree to which we understand ourselves, the impact of our origins and upbringing, and specifically our early feelings and reactions to team membership.

It is important to manage these feelings successfully. We need to be able to respond to the feedback and signals that others give us and behave appropriately and confidently in the team context. For some of us this will feel as natural as it does for a fish to swim; for others it may require more conscious effort, and perhaps the help of trusted colleagues – or a coach – to talk things through. As we gain knowledge and develop skill in regard to ourselves we should also become increasingly aware of the impact of team dynamics on our colleagues – especially the fact that we each experience these dynamics differently. And remember that, whilst you are responding to the team and its individual members, they are experiencing their own response, conscious or otherwise, to you. This is never more important than when you first join.

Making the right impact

In the early 1980s I was working in a local authority children's assessment centre, in charge of a unit that cared for fifteen teenage boys who had been placed in care, mostly in very difficult circumstances. We also made arrangements for their social, educational and psychiatric assessment. We ran a happy and well-disciplined unit with a cohesive team of staff. Standards were set high and we prided ourselves on being smart, punctual and professional in the way we worked together. One day I was expecting a temporary member of staff on extended loan from another establishment in the borough. He eventually arrived, but a couple of hours late, having left us short-handed for the morning's work. I remember opening the door to him: he sauntered in wearing shorts and t-shirt, a huge tape-player slung over his shoulder. He smiled broadly, addressed me as 'mate' and immediately found himself a comfortable chair. I briefly considered telling him to leave but was desperate for the extra hands. As it turned out he was a pleasant, clever and capable man and, after we had had a couple of purposeful conversations, he settled well into the team. However, his initial impact was such that at first the team took against him; it took him far longer to settle in and gain acceptance than necessary; and one or two members of the team continued to harbour doubts about him for the rest of his time with us.

When you join a team the very first moments of your arrival carry massive impact. For this impact to be in your favour you need to consider:

- What is the overall culture of this team and of its surrounding organisation?
- What are the rules or conventions of dress I need to take into account?
- What is the level of formality/informality?
- How are things done here?
- Which behaviours gain social approval and which disapproval?
- What values are in evidence in the way people talk and behave?
- What is the basic rhythm and energy of the team?

In short you need to concentrate on developing rapport at all levels whilst maintaining your own sense of identity and character – a balancing act. The key to handling this phase is to establish clear goals about the impression you want to create. First impressions really do count and last for a long time.

Meanwhile you need to consider your long-term goals – what role would you like to play in the team? This is likely to involve a consideration of your personal values – what you believe is right about how people should behave and work together. Ultimately your values reflect what you stand for as a person – and what you won't stand for too!

Gaining entry

The first few weeks as a new member of a team can be a very testing time. With luck you will be welcomed and supported. But you may find yourself subject to the egos and selfish interests of certain of your new team mates just as you are trying to find your feet. Looking back on the professional teams I have joined myself, I can recall some subtle – and some absolutely blatant – attempts to keep me in my place and exert dominance. These have included:

- Being told, literally, that the 'new boy' was expected to make the tea (I was 26 at the time and joining a team as a senior social worker)
- Having someone take a dessert off my tray at lunch on my first day because he wanted it and it was the last one left!
- Hearing that in order to 'get on' in the team it would be advisable for me to listen a lot and say little
- Being told by a peer that I *had* to work in a particular way
- Having decisions made as part of a leadership team overturned unilaterally by a colleague on the grounds that he 'knew' he was 'right'
- Being asked to do extremely difficult and unpleasant work that others did not want to do

I wish I could report I had handled each of these with confidence and skill, but they probably stand out in my memory because I handled them unsuccessfully. I made the tea; I had a flaring row with the pudding-pincher, and so on.

There is no doubt that this can be a highly challenging phase. Courage can be a key factor in facing up to those who seek to test you with their behaviour. A tendency for self-deprecating humour can take you a long way. Handling the so-called small-talk well can give you a flying start – listening, summarising and asking open questions about your colleagues will give them a chance to talk about themselves, which most people enjoy. It is also useful to think about a firm policy for handling contingencies that may arise.

Checking for hot spots

We are all capable of being taken by surprise by the strength of our own reactions to something. A colleague adopts the wrong tone or touches inadvertently on an area where you feel vulnerable or sensitive – an emotional hot spot – and you over-react. The impact on your relationship with the colleague or on your standing in the team can last for a long time. It is better to reflect in advance on such hot spots than to find yourself hijacked by a negative response. Self-control must be balanced, however, by the need to be spontaneous and authentic: no one can sustain any kind of act convincingly for more than a short time so it is important to be your real self, ideally your real self at its best.

Over the past ten or fifteen years the concept of *Emotional Intelligence* has assumed increasing importance in organisational life. Recognition has grown that ultimate career potential depends on being able to conduct oneself well in terms of managing oneself and managing relationships with others. This means:

- Understanding yourself – your makeup, personality, drivers, strengths and weaknesses
- Managing yourself effectively – your well-being, stress levels, motivation and social behaviour
- Understanding others – especially recognising that we vary enormously in how we experience the world and how we choose to express ourselves in it
- Managing relationships effectively – negotiating all the complexities of life in an organisation

Each of these factors is vital to the whole process of joining in a team, finding your feet and settling in to both the formal and informal aspects of your team role. Of course, emotional intelligence is not a subject that confines itself to team membership; it is a vital asset in all aspects of professional life, and one cannot operate effectively as a team leader or team coach without it. Psychologist Daniel Goleman, who developed the concept, does not consider an individual's emotional intelligence to be a fixed value (Goleman, 1996). Practical ways of actively developing your abilities in this area can be found in *Working with Emotional Intelligence* (Goleman, 1999).

Being assertive

As important as managing ourselves is learning to manage colleagues, particularly those who attempt to dominate or who make unreasonable requests. Assertiveness as a topic of management education has something of an old-fashioned feel to it. Partly this is due to the way in which it was sometimes taught in the 1980s and 1990s, with an emphasis on rigid phraseology that did not carry either conviction or authenticity. The phrase 'I hear what you are saying . . .' for example, whilst supposedly intended to convey an attitude of respectful attentiveness, was almost invariably followed with a 'but . . .' and a counter argument. Similarly the phrase 'with respect . . .' was frequently the signal for an outright insult. Some of the vocabulary of assertiveness therefore fell into disrepute, and with it, to some degree, the whole concept. Partly it was because the formulaic approach of teaching specific phraseology did not allow sufficient flexibility or variation for handling different kinds of people in a wide variety of contexts. Rapport could be jeopardised by the use of these phrases. Richard Bandler, co-creator of Neuro-Linguistic Programming (NLP), once said he thought that 'assertiveness training' should be re-named 'loneliness preparation' (Bandler, 1985).

However, the real value of the assertiveness proposition lies in its underpinning principles rather than in any specific phraseology. This core principle is:

Respect your own needs and rights and at the same time respect the needs and rights of other people.

This is a sound principle as long as one does not assume that everyone else likes to be treated exactly as we do ourselves. This golden rule is outdated and should be replaced with 'Treat others as they themselves wish to be treated'. This is even more important in an increasingly multicultural society where behavioural norms are diverse. The specific techniques described below need to be regarded with this point in mind. They are useful in many contexts, not just that of team membership.

Saying 'no' effectively

Learning to say no is essential if you want to avoid being overloaded with inappropriate and unsatisfying tasks. You will enjoy your work more, progress faster and contribute more effectively to the team if you are able to exercise some judgement over the use of your time. Saying no can be a tough skill in any context – not least for leaders of teams. However tough we may appear to be it can be difficult to say no to someone, especially a team colleague. We may not want to disappoint them, we may feel that if we say no we will attract unpopularity or we may feel we risk getting a reputation within the team as being unsupportive or uncooperative. Even if we *do* feel comfortable with the need to refuse a request it does not follow that we do so skilfully, in a way that preserves or, better still, enhances the quality of the relationship – the benchmark of all good influencing skills. Typical mistakes in saying no include:

- Never actually bringing ourselves to say the word – instead using weak and ambiguous phrases such as 'Gosh, I'd like to say yes, but it's a little difficult' or 'I'll need to think about that – can you come back to me?'

- Not owning the decision to say no, instead laying responsibility on others, e.g. 'I'd like to say yes, but I don't think my boss would like it.'
- Being over-aggressive and abrupt, just saying 'no' without any reason or sign of concern for the other person
- Over-explaining – saying 'no' but offering so many reasons that at least one of them is going to appear weak and therefore give the person making the request every encouragement to argue or to ask again

The trick is to say no in such a way that you appear simultaneously strong, reasonable, respectful and flexible. To this end it is worth developing a format that you can rely on in a wide range of contexts. Here is a basic template that many people have found useful:

1   Use the person's name and summarise the request, thus showing you have been listening, e.g. 'OK John, so you want me to stand in for you at the operations meeting this afternoon so that you can prepare for your project presentation next week.'
2   Turn down the request clearly without any equivocation, using 'I', e.g. 'John, I am afraid I am going to have to say no to this one.'
3   Give just *one* good reason, e.g. 'I have a pressing appointment that I really can't break.'
4   Show some flexibility and willingness to be helpful without giving way, e.g. 'But let's look at some other way I can help you find some time later on in the week.'

If the other person comes back with a repeat request, simply start again from the point at which you say no. It is important to stick with your original reason. Offering two or three more reasons when someone persists in their request will sooner or later throw up a reason that is weak and easier to argue with. Remember that if your original reason is legitimate and not just an excuse, there is no need to find new reasons. Stay friendly, but use the broken record technique until they realise you mean business.

For the person saying no, this can feel daunting. But experience and feedback tell me that saying no clearly and politely often earns more respect than evading the issue or fudging it with a weak answer. I would suggest practising the format until it becomes easy to use.

Asking for what you want

Just as important in establishing some control over the circumstances of your working life is the ability to make legitimate requests. This is a similar skill to saying no and can feel as awkward. The key is to make sure that what you are asking for is reasonable and justified. Ask clearly and unambiguously for what you want, offering one reason for your request and giving plenty of room for the other person to respond. Do not get drawn into offering secondary reasons, but stick to your guns. Be prepared to listen to reasonable alternatives and demonstrate that you are willing to help, without compromising on your essential requirements. A good sequence might look like this:

1 Address the person by name.
2 State your request straightforwardly, using the word 'I'. Don't wander around the issue, wrapping it up with ifs and buts or attributing the request to others.
3 Invite comments and solutions.
4 If appropriate offer reasons for what you are asking.

Giving feedback

If you are to hold your own as a team member and play a full part in the team's collective performance, you may need to give feedback to a colleague. This often requires courage and should always be done with sensitivity and skill. The key to doing this effectively is to leave the recipient with choice about how to respond. Consider how you might feel if someone said to you something like:

'You are being so negative! You really need to step up to the plate!'

Feedback in this form is vague and generalised; it offers a judgemental viewpoint and an instruction to change. You are likely to feel put down and resistant. If the feedback was handled in the following way you would probably feel differently:

'Could I offer you some feedback? I have noticed that when we get towards the point of tying down some actions you tend to go quiet and shake your head. The impact on me is to make me wonder if you are convinced we are going down the right road. It would help me to know what you are really thinking on these occasions so that I can take your thinking into consideration.'

Feedback in this form is non-judgemental – it describes behaviour without judging it. The recipient is left with a choice over how to respond. Furthermore when someone says how they feel it is hard to disagree with them whereas you may often disagree with someone's judgement or interpretation of your behaviour.

When giving feedback:

• Ask permission – it is rarely refused
• Describe the behaviour in literal terms without judging it
• Describe the impact of the behaviour on you
• Ask for what you would like to be different

Feedback should not be about dumping, blaming or generalising. Timing is important too – offering feedback when the other person is upset or flustered is unlikely to help. On the other hand, feedback left too late is likely to have little impact.

Even under these conditions, feedback can only really succeed if you are in a calm, open frame of mind and intend to instigate a productive discussion. Handled well it can be wonderfully productive in creating better relationships and avoiding some of the tense stalemates colleagues can get into if they do not discuss behavioural issues that affect them.

Getting clarity on your role

Lack of role clarity is a powerful stress factor for individuals in the workplace. Overall team effectiveness is also highly dependent on each member being clear on exactly what is expected of them in terms of responsibilities, performance and behaviour. Some team leaders are much more effective than others at managing individual performance. Performance management systems (in which annual objectives are set) are often afforded little more than lip-service. You may need to take individual responsibility for ensuring you know exactly what is expected of you. If in doubt, arrange a meeting with your boss to discuss:

- Key aspects of your role in specific terms, and how your role fits in with those of your team mates
- Key indicators of performance – what is really expected of you – including measures or, failing that, indicators of success, such as what others should be seeing, hearing and feeling about your performance
- Feedback on your current performance and what improvements the boss would like to see
- Development targets – what you and your boss agree you should aim to be learning in addition to your current skills and knowledge

Wilfred Bion, a British Army psychologist, conducted groundbreaking and influential research during and after the Second World War on the psychology of groups (Bion, 1968). One of his most important contributions was the realisation that a group needed *significant shared purpose* if it were to avoid falling into negative psychological patterns associated with insecurity. These negative patterns would include leadership struggles and sub-group bonding or clique-building.

A look at modern reality TV shows such as *Big Brother* bears this out: participants sit around for most of the time lethargically generating emotional toxicity, until some kind of task or challenge is introduced, at which point the group invariably perks up and behaves with purpose and energy. Once the task is completed, the group relapses into relationship and power struggles. The hyper-real intensity of the reality shows is an accurate reflection of some of the key components of Bion's work.

As a team member your influence on the shared sense of purpose will be limited, but you can at least take responsibility for identifying and fulfilling your own role and key performance goals.

Playing to your strengths

We are not all the same in our social and interpersonal needs or in our preferred ways of working. Given that we rarely choose our team colleagues, it is vital that we have insight into how other people manage and express their individual characteristics and interpersonal needs. It is just as important, if we are to find effective and satisfying roles, that we understand something of our own strengths and preferences – how we work best alongside others and how we like to be treated.

An excellent starting point is a psychometric tool called FIRO-B. FIRO-B is short for 'Fundamental Interpersonal Relationships Orientation – Behaviour'. This unwieldy mouthful of a title belies an elegant and deceptively simple approach to understanding your social needs and preferences – and those of others. Essentially it helps you clarify what you really want from others in social situations, how you might come across to them, and how you might better handle your relationships at work and elsewhere. It is popularly in use in team development sessions and is rated as one of the most respected and research-validated instruments in the world. FIRO-B also offers a thorough framework of understanding into how interpersonal conflicts can occur – and how to prevent them occurring. Ideally this should be administered and explained by a licensed practitioner but a very good basic understanding can be gained by reading and by taking an online questionnaire at www. advancedpeoplestrategies.co.uk. In response you will receive a report from a company called APS. In addition I would recommend *Introduction to the FIRO-B Instrument* by Judith Waterman and Jenny Rogers – a simply-written and authoritative book (Waterman and Rogers, 1996).

Another way of understanding your 'fit' in teams is to look at the Belbin's theory of team roles (Belbin, 1981). This is explained in more detail in Chapter 4. Essentially the Belbin Team Role Inventory examines which of a set of *informal* team roles – roles that fall outside your explicit job-description – is most natural to you. It can be immensely helpful to recognise that are many equally legitimate ways of contributing to the work of a team; that the team is likely to be more effective, in fact, if its members have different but complementary strengths. It is possible to purchase individual questionnaires from Belbin at www.belbin.com. For about £30 you can purchase an individual report form which allows you to self-assess and to incorporate the views of your team mates.

There are numerous other audits and psychometrics that relate strongly to team membership. Perhaps the best known in the coaching and business world is the Myers-Briggs Type Inventory (MBTI). This is a rigorously validated psychometric instrument that many teams use to examine the interplay of different personality types. Founded on the psychological theories of Carl Jung (Jung, 1991), it reflects human variety in a rich and complex way. In my experience it can be somewhat bewildering if not skilfully presented. I have encountered many people who have been briefly exposed to it and retain a simplistic or erroneous view of it. An excellent introduction is a short book called *Sixteen Personality Types* by Jenny Rogers (Rogers, 2007).

I have recently been introduced to an instrument called Realise2. This is a questionnaire designed by the Centre for Applied Positive Psychology (CAPP), which was founded in 2005 by Alex Linley. The positive psychology movement, which originated in the late 1990s in the work of Martin Seligman and Mihaly Csikszentmihalyi, focuses on 'positive human functioning' (Seligman and Csikszentmihalyi (2000)). Its practitioners are interested in verifiable interventions that will help individuals and communities to thrive. Though some have unfairly criticised it for what they see as its gung-ho optimism, positive psychology is gaining credibility as a school of thought. Realise2 draws on research evidence to determine your key personal and professional strengths whilst making a distinction between the strengths you have that *energise* you and those strengths that *drain* you. This can provide valuable insights into the sources of your own sense of well-being and fulfilment, as distinct from your value to your boss or your team. There is full analysis of your key strengths, and guidance as to how to use them effectively. It costs about £15 at time of writing to use the questionnaire online and is available at www.cappeu.com.

Getting support and managing your development

It is essential to have access to personal support and this can come in several forms. If you are lucky, *your boss* will be a source of encouragement and guidance, although we all know bosses who are weak in this area or who do not see this as part of their role. A good boss should be available for one-to-one meetings on a regular basis. Ideally this will include time for you and your professional development as well as for the discussion of work. Similarly a good boss will keep on track of your progress against objectives and be able to offer support if for any reasons these objectives fall off target; performance management should be more than just an annual appraisal. Not every boss is going to be ideal in this respect. Research published recently by the Gallup organisation shows that across the world and across all demographics the least nurturing relationship you are likely to have in your life is with your boss (Rath and Harter, 2010).

Your *colleagues* could be a valuable source of support and comradeship. Some teams have a form of 'buddy' system in which a new team member is allocated an informal mentor who can help you navigate the early stages of a new job. Some have a pairing system in which an individual colleague commits to providing ongoing support.

Formal mentoring is available in many organisations – although the amount of investment in training mentors varies considerably. A mentor is not normally part of an immediate work team but someone more senior who has been in the organisation for some time. They should offer a confidential service that can help you to:

- Understand the culture of the organisation
- Navigate the political aspects of organisational life
- Discuss issues concerning your team or your boss
- Network with other key members of the organisation
- Get a wider view of your own development

A coach can be exceptionally helpful in enabling you to function well in a team, particularly in the early stages of team membership. Some business coaches are sourced externally, particularly at the executive level, and others are part of internal coaching schemes. A coach generally works as an equal partner in a non-advisory role, specialising in careful listening and focused questioning to help you think through issues chosen by you. Coaching has developed a strong reputation over the past ten to fifteen years, and whereas initially a coaching intervention may have been seen as something remedial it is now becoming firmly established as a desirable developmental tool. A good mentor can also use coaching skills.

A counsellor may be an option in instances where you are experiencing personal difficulty, especially with emotional issues such as relationship problems or with some aspects of mental health. Many organisations offer at least some access to counselling as part of a staff welfare scheme.

Whilst support may be available from most if not all of these sources it may not be supplied automatically. Be prepared to ask. If you feel you need specialist support such as coaching, be ready to make a case for it. Do not assume that your team will necessarily be focused on your welfare – in my work with teams I have sometimes found it is not unusual for individuals in teams to undergo a serious personal trauma or career crisis without anyone else in the team even being aware of it.

Offering support to others

One way of being a good team player is to set out actively to support your colleagues. You can do this *informally* – for example, by keeping alert for any signs of stress in your team mates and offering to help by listening and chatting things through – or *formally* – for example, by offering to 'buddy' a new colleague or by acting as a peer coach. If no such schemes are established in your team you could be the one to suggest starting something up.

Dealing with conflict in teams effectively

In any team there is likely to be some kind of conflict. One key indicator of a well-functioning team is that conflict is handled skilfully and maturely. Conflict can be a positive if it is seen as a means of learning and bridge-building. Healthy conflict will focus on work issues – for example, how to get things done better – rather than on personal issues. A personality clash can drain the energy from a team, either erupting in damaging anger and aggression or festering away as unspoken rivalry, tension or disagreement. One avenue for developing a positive role and a reputation as a team player is to develop your own conflict management skills to a high level.

A good start point for this would be to look at the Thomas Kilmann Conflict Mode Instrument (TKI). This can be helpful in building awareness of your own attitude to conflict and your preferred means of dealing with it. The instrument looks at two key behavioural/attitudinal dimensions in particular, *competitiveness* and *cooperation*. The instrument is based on the theory that we each have a preferred or habitual style in dealing with conflict and offers ways of understanding when other styles may be more appropriate.

No training is required to use or administer TKI. For more information visit www.opp.eu.com. Materials and reading matter are available for purchase and you can take a short quiz based on the full instrument that can help you to understand how well you are dealing with conflict currently.

Performing effectively in meetings and creating positive impact

In my work as an executive coach, I am constantly being asked for help in managing positive personal impact. This can apply to a wide range of scenarios including preparation for interviews, making presentations, and – a perennial subject – performing well in meetings. Two factors common to these situations are the need for confidence and the importance of planning effectively. In order to handle yourself well in a meeting it is important to:

- Arrive on time, prepared, understanding the agenda.
- Focus on the *outcomes* you are looking for under agenda items that concern you rather than anticipating problems that might arise during the meeting. A problem focus can drain energy away from what you are trying to achieve and express itself in negative body language.
- Listen actively to others, attending to what is significant in what they say and using summary to show you have listened.
- When advocating your own view, keep it simple and offer only the strongest one or two points in support of your case. Repeat what you have said rather than look for supplementary, weaker points.
- Make your advocacy even more potent by looking for opportunities to include narrative in your presentations or when arguing your case. We are hard wired neurologically to listen to stories and story-telling is the most potent of all persuasion techniques.
- Make your thought process 'visible'. If you make a proposal, back it up by saying what thinking has led you to your view. This makes it much easier for members of the meeting to understand where you are coming from.
- Look for ways of offering genuine compromise when there is disagreement, without sacrificing your own legitimate interests. One useful negotiating tactic is to offer something that is relatively easy for you to give, in return for something you really need or want.
- Look for ways to support your colleagues on issues of importance to them.

Managing your time

Working as one of a team commonly involves juggling many different tasks and coordinating a variety of deadlines. The competing demands on your time can be overwhelming, unless you are organised. One useful organising tool is the 'Urgent/Important Matrix' originally developed by S.R. Covey in 1989 (Covey, 2004). The essence of this is to understand where your time and energy delivers the best value and the most sustainable, healthy work pattern.

In broad outline, this is how a representative example of the matrix might look:

Important not urgent	*Urgent and important*
• Prevention	• Crises
• Planning	• Emergencies
• Relationship building	• Deadline driven projects

(Continued)

• Strategic/Creative thinking • Personal development	• Urgent demands for information • Fire fighting

Not urgent not important	*Urgent not important*

• Trivia
• Pleasant activities
• Some mail
• Some emails
• Some phone calls
	• Some phone calls
	• Some demands for
	  information
	• Some ad hoc conversations
	• Meetings that only
	  marginally concern you

Different people will necessarily populate these categories with different things, but as a rule of thumb:

- Too much time in the *urgent and important* area may lead to stress and burnout.
- Significant time spent in the *important not urgent* area should lead to a sense of control, balance perspective and discipline.
- Too much time in the *urgent not important* area can lead to short termism, a sense of being out of control and feeling harassed or even persecuted.
- Any significant time spent in the *not urgent not important* area can be seen as irresponsible and irrelevant.

In thinking about your own job, you can use this matrix to manage your time and energy to your own benefit, while enhancing the value of your contribution to the team.

Managing your boss

A lot is written in articles on management about this subject, some of it contradictory and much of it openly manipulative and self-serving. A lot depends on specific circumstances and the level of seniority at which you are operating. Here are a few minimum standards to aspire to in terms of keeping your boss onside and supportive of you:

- Do what you say you are going to do in order to breed confidence and trust.
- Develop expertise or knowledge that the boss needs but does not have.

- Be prepared to show integrity by standing up for what you believe even when the boss disagrees with you.
- If the boss's decision goes against you accept it and do not moan to others about it.
- Focus on solutions rather than problems.
- Demonstrate that your work is helping to achieve the boss's goals.
- Show some interest in the boss as a person.

Precisely what strategies you employ will depend on what type of boss you are dealing with. Here are some examples of types who will need to be managed with particular skill:

The micro-manager can be very hard to satisfy and can seem to be interfering and overbearing. In addition to the guidelines above you may need to be prepared to keep them in the loop with regular information and reassurance. Additionally you may want to offer feedback which shows you need less supervision and more freedom – handle this with tact! When you are answerable to a micro-manager it is important to ensure you have been delegated to in a clear way with specific goals and that you have been given the authority as well as the responsibility for achieving them – avoid at all costs being put in a situation where you have all the responsibility and no authority.

The absent boss who is focused on managing upwards may be focused on keeping a high political profile or representing the team's interests in the wider organisation. Ensure you have regular, routine meetings booked with them so you are not forever trying to squeeze yourself into their diary. In addition, keep yourself abreast of the wider organisation's policies and issues in order to understand what your boss is dealing with.

The toxic or bullying boss – sadly still exists, often in sheep's clothing. There are really only three main options here if feedback about their behaviour fails to effect a change:

- Confront them with their behaviour – and be prepared to move on if necessary.
- Refer their behaviour to an internal Human Resources representative, to a union official or to an external agency such as the UK National Workplace Bullying Advice Line – www.bullyonline.org – which is also a good source of information on workplace bullying in general.
- Leave before confronting them and before your health and well-being is jeopardised.

These choices may seem stark but there is a great deal of evidence to show the negative effect of a toxic boss. Bullying remains a serious issue in the workplace and a lot of it stays underground with serious consequences for its victims.

Summary

Should the scenarios and warnings above seem a little forbidding, remember that teams can be great fun to work in and you can develop lasting friendships as well as on-the-job camaraderie. Even if your FIRO-B scores tell you that you have a low need for social inclusion you should include yourself in at least *some* of the social activities that are generally on offer in a reasonably healthy team. Building social bonds is an end in itself but can also enhance the richness of the work experience and help a team to generate true team spirit – an essential ingredient of performance. A well-functioning team can provide a rewarding, even exhilarating context for work. By taking the time to prepare yourself to be a good colleague and to function well in a work team you can significantly enrich your job satisfaction and enhance your career prospects – so many job adverts now ask for evidence that you are a 'good team player'.

Key learning points

- For your own development and to ensure you get the best out of your involvement in teams it is important to learn as much about yourself as possible. Investigating some of the learning on offer from the various psychometric instruments available and from other relevant questionnaires can be a powerful way of doing this, particularly if you get the opportunity to work through them with a competent coach. Understanding yourself is the root of all wisdom and a key factor in developing emotional intelligence.
- Never underestimate the value of first impressions: take steps to manage your immediate impact when you join a new team.
- As part of this preparation create a policy for yourself that encompasses how you want to be seen in both the long term and the short term and which incorporates how you might deal with behaviours from others that touches your emotional hot spots.
- Follow the *principles* of assertiveness rather than its clichéd phraseology.
- Practise how to say no, ask for what you want and give effective feedback.
- Make sure you gain clarity about what is expected of you at an early stage.
- Make the effort to learn more about yourself as the basis for developing emotional intelligence.
- Assume responsibility for your own development – do not leave it to chance.
- Look to be a good team member by supporting your colleagues and your boss.

Reflective questions

- Think about teams you have been a member of up until now – which have been your favourites and why? What does this say about the kinds of team you might most benefit from being a member of going forward?
- What are your core strengths as a team player – especially those that *energise* you? How can you find opportunities to work to these strengths?
- What are the areas arising from this chapter you may need to work most on?

2 Essential skills for team leaders and coaches

'In theory there is no difference between theory and practice. But in practice, there is.'

– attributed to Yogi Berra

There is less clarity and consensus about what a team coach does than there is about individual coaching of the type most usually referred to as executive coaching. This applies as much to the manager who employs coaching behaviours with his or her own team as to the 'specialist' independent team coach. Some who are described as team coaches are in reality primarily facilitators or team-builders.

David Clutterbuck, one of a few authors who have attempted to create more clarity about the role, observes that there are very few academic studies of coaching teams at work; that evaluation of team coaching is in fact in its infancy lagging behind what is a growing body of research on executive or managerial one-to-one coaching (Clutterbuck, 2007). He points out that there are many different types of team and these differences require a flexible approach. There are also different kinds of team coach, from the manager or leader who coaches, to the independent coach hired to coach leadership teams. In Clutterbuck's view, there is often confusion about what is team coaching and what is merely facilitation or team-building. He argues that a team coach who is more than just a facilitator needs more than the competencies of a one-to-one coach, requiring also a sound understanding of team dynamics based on both direct experience and theoretical study.

As yet there is no clear consensus as to the nature of the team coach's role and no obvious limit to the skill and knowledge a team coach might acquire. In this chapter I will lay out what I consider to be the essential skills and knowledge and point also to some desirable areas for learning.

What is team coaching?

At a minimum, a team coach is someone who works with a team over a period of time to:

- Support it in learning and growing
- Enable it to access its full potential
- Build performance capability and capacity
- Overcome challenges and obstacles to progress
- Help it achieve clarity of purpose, goals, values and working methods
- Work through changes of membership or leadership
- Help it adapt to organisational change

A team coach needs the skills and knowledge to:

- Facilitate team discussions
- Coach one-to-one, using executive coaching skills in a team context
- Use process consulting skills to analyse and describe team issues within an organisational context
- Design and lead an array of events and activities to meet a wide variety of individual team requirements
- Be familiar with a wide range of relevant theoretical models
- Have the judgement and experience to make good choices about the mix and timing of all such elements

The personal qualities needed

Some of the qualities needed to coach teams are attributes of experience and character rather than anything that can be acquired through book learning alone. Team coaching involves more than just 'one-off' interventions; the coach may need to work with a team for months or even years, dealing with them at their most sensitive, raw and dramatic moments. At the heart of any such extended encounter lies a set of deeply human relationships that at times can test the personal resources and character of the team coach to the limit. Theoretical knowledge alone will not buy you the respect, commitment and trust of teams and their leaders who are often working under extreme pressure, who are frequently suspicious of anything that smacks even remotely of 'consultant speak' and who will rarely suffer fools gladly. There is probably no ideal profile, but minimally a team coach needs:

- The ability to be assertive in a way that always conveys human respect and support

- The flexibility to be able to create rapport with a very wide range of personality types and across many kinds of cultural context
- A strongly developed attitude of respect for a wide range of cultures, combined with the ability to behave acceptably within them whilst not compromising core personal values
- A strong sense of humour – particularly about oneself. This is not a role for the precious!
- The ability to both plan methodically and have the flexibility to respond to contingency
- An active working belief in the resourcefulness of people, translating to an assumption that no matter what the difficulties, the team can succeed; that they have the resources they need to make the progress they desire
- High personal confidence and resilience – physical and emotional
- The ability to think clearly and calmly under pressure
- The ability to handle ambiguity, loose ends and uncertainty
- High integrity and a commitment to behaving in a trustworthy way
- High political intelligence – the ability to read a situation and know how to handle it with judgement and discretion
- Sensitivity to group and individual mood
- A detachment from one's own need for affection, inclusion and control in a team context
- Goal focus – the ability to always keep sight of the end goal
- 'Centredness' – a strong capability to maintain internal equilibrium anchored by clear values

Certainly, experience helps. Situations that can seem alarming or even threatening when one is new to working intensely with teams seem much less so as experience builds. It is reassuring to be familiar with techniques, models and processes that can genuinely help guide you through the potential minefield of group behaviour. As your confidence grows so will teams you work with grow more confident in you – in itself an important constituent of success.

Learning about the team

A common start point for a team coaching intervention is to follow this process:

1   Interview each member of the team to determine their views (see sample protocol for this below).
2   Interview key stakeholders for the team to determine how the team is viewed from the outside.

3   Write a non-attributable report that summarises the key findings of the interviews.
4   Write a suggested beginning of a team coaching process, such as an outline for a first day together.
5   Distribute the report and invite comment both on the report and the recommendations for the programme.
6   Adjust the report and the recommendations in the light of any comments received.

A core skill that the team coach needs is to be able to conduct appropriate diagnostic interviews with team members. A typical process is to have preliminary discussions with the team leader (who is often the instigator of a team coaching intervention). This preliminary discussion is an important part of the whole process and would normally involve the following questions:

- What is the issue with the team that needs to be addressed? Is it a problem or a development issue?
- What, in broad terms, do you need from a team coaching intervention?
- What evidence will you look for to judge if the intervention has been successful?
- Are there any potentially sensitive issues that the team coach needs to be aware of?
- Who is the main point of contact and sponsor for this intervention?
- Who are the key stakeholders of this exercise and what authority or influence do they have?

When going on to interview individual members of the team some alternative questions are useful. Here is a selection:

- In general terms, how would you describe the working atmosphere or climate of the team?
- Describe the team working at its best . . .
- Describe the team working at its worst . . .
- What is your formal role within the team?
- What informal roles do you play within the team?
- How would you describe the leadership of the team?
- How would you describe the team's interaction and relationships with other teams and key stakeholders?
- How effective are the team's processes – meetings, communications, working practices?
- How proud is the team of itself and of its work?
- How much attention is paid to standards and to achievement?
- How are people recognised and rewarded?

- How much responsibility and accountability are team members given?
- What 'elephants in the room' are there?
- What must this team development process achieve for you personally if it is to have value?
- What do you *not* want the team process to do?
- What would be your advice to me as a team coach if I am to be successful?
- How could the whole process be sabotaged?
- How will we avoid such sabotage happening?

It should be explained clearly to each member of the team that when you speak to them individually you will respect confidentiality. Your purpose is to collect information to provide the basis of a thematic report setting out key issues the team needs to address.

On the basis of what the team members say you can write a report with a suggested outline 'schedule of works' for a team development process. I would suggest that you keep the report short – no more than two pages. Focus on the key issues on which performance and effectiveness depend. Issue the report to everyone in the team, by prior agreement with the leader. Offer a draft agenda for the first meeting only – whilst indicating other development activities that may be useful further down the line. Ask for comments on both the report and the suggested agenda before finalising either.

Contracting

In the context of team coaching, a contract is an agreed statement about how the team is going to work together. It should cover specific behaviours and attitudes that the team agrees will be essential to progress and learning. It should include something about what the team members expect of each other, what they expect of the team coach and what the team coach expects from the team. It should be written up, re-visited from time to time and perhaps revised as the team coaching assignment progresses.

Contracting is a skill that is important in every aspect of the team coach's role. A good contract is the glue that holds together the whole process and therefore needs careful construction at the outset. I have seen this handled in a rather dreary and dutiful way on courses or at the first full session, the coach or trainer diminishing its significance with a phrase such as 'let's just agree the ground rules then'.

My own view is that a contract is only likely to be really useful if it is predicated on an expectation of success and sufficiently specific in describing behaviours and situations. Simply putting up a list of bullet-pointed clichés on a flip chart is unlikely to be helpful.

An approach I have found both stimulating and relatively simple is this:

- Ask the team members to envisage a *successful* outcome to the team coaching intervention – regardless of what they feel about the team in the present. Get them to imagine walking away from the final session in the knowledge that the team has benefited hugely from the process and is much stronger and more effective as a result.
- Ask them to look back, in their imaginations, from this position of future success, to *how* the programme achieved such success (some may struggle a bit with this but usually they get it with a little encouragement).
- Ask them: '*How* did we achieve this? What did we do – or not do – that made us successful?'
- Write down their initial responses, which are likely to be generalisations, on the left hand side of a flip chart.
- When you have finished this, ask them to expand on what they have said: for example, if someone says, 'We were open and honest', ask them for specific examples of what this would mean in practice.

The flip chart might look something like this:

Success factors	Specific examples
We were open and honest	• When we disagreed we said so openly rather than just keeping it to ourselves • We offered our views even if they were at odds with what other people in the team thought • We gave genuine feedback to each other even if it was tough
We treated each other with respect	• We valued each other's contributions as genuine efforts to contribute even if we did not agree with each other • We listened genuinely before offering our own views
We managed conflict effectively	• When we disagreed we took a constructive and positive approach to finding solutions we could all live with • We agreed that conflict was a necessary part of healthy team functioning as long as it was directed at work and not personal issues
We looked for creative solutions	• We consciously made space for creativity in finding ways forward • We practised techniques such as brainstorming in which all contributions were elicited before they were evaluated

It is important in this contracting process to include something about expectations on what the team coach is going to do or not do. Typical offerings include things like 'Keep us on track' or 'Hold us to account for our behaviour', and again it is important to get some specific examples of what this might mean in practice.

Finally it is vital that the contract, once agreed, remains a live document. It can be reviewed at regular intervals and adjusted as required. When contracting is skimped or neglected altogether it can come back to bite you. A good contract is at the heart of managing team process and behaviour.

Creating rapport

> 'Tain't what you do it's the way that you do it.'
> – Melvin 'Sy' Oliver and James 'Trummy' Young

Rapport is hugely important in all human relations, and the ability to develop and maintain an authentic rapport with a wide range of individuals, both one-to-one and in groups, is an absolute must for the team coach and team leader. Without such skills it is virtually impossible to work effectively in either role. At the heart of being able to develop rapport skilfully and with integrity is a genuine desire to make effective communication coupled with an attitude of respect for others. Also required is an intellectual conviction that how we personally see the world is not how others see, interpret and experience it, and that the world views of others are as valid as our own. Emotional and behavioural flexibility is needed, as is the ability to tune in to someone else and respond to them quickly. We also need to understand that most of the behaviour that influences us – and by which we influence others – is both generated and received at an unconscious level. Finally, we need the humility to recognise that if what we are doing to create rapport is not working, it is time to stop doing it and try something else.

Rapport building happens ultimately through the use of skilful physical and linguistic behaviours. Each requires the underpinning of the attitudes and beliefs described above if they are to be genuinely effective.

Matching body language

This is probably the most popularly known and most frequently derided technique aimed at creating rapport. Casual observers are often keen to describe it as superficial and manipulative, but practised with integrity it can build over time into a seamless social skill that can help to set up positive relationships from the word go, regardless of issues of race, culture or status. The essence of the skill is:

1   Pay immediate initial attention to the other person – notice how they are presenting physically.

2   *Match:* adapt your body language (posture, gesture, expression, pace, energy) so that it becomes more like theirs.

3   *Pace:* maintain the closer match for a period.

4   *Lead:* as and when necessary, change your behaviour to something that may be more desirable in the moment. For example, adopt a more energised and alert posture if the other person's energy seems low for an undesirably lengthy period. If you have matched and paced effectively the other person is likely to follow you towards a more resourceful state.

This is not just aping or mimicry – which would indeed be superficial and probably disrespectful – but simply an opportunity to set the right tone for a relationship from the outset. We make up our minds about each other at an unconscious level very quickly and once someone makes a negative judgement in their minds about us it is very hard to win them over. Job interviewers for example are notoriously prone to make snap judgements about interviewees – and once that judgement is made it usually sticks no matter how long the interview goes on. Matching gives us the chance to make the first few critical seconds of any meeting positive.

One of the beauties of this matching technique is that it gets away from the vexed issue of body language interpretation. This is particularly important in cross-cultural situations, where implicit cultural assumptions can lead to incorrect judgements about the meaning of particular behaviours in people from different cultures. For example, received wisdom on the importance of keeping steady eye contact may work well in the white populations of the UK, Canada, Australia, South Africa and the USA (where most of the influential studies on body language were conducted) but there are other cultures where it can be seen as intrusive or rude. In some cultures close physical proximity is seen as the norm, in others keeping distance is more acceptable, and so on.

By following the matching technique you do someone the courtesy of showing them at an unconscious level your intention to reflect back something of how they express themselves. It is only manipulative if your *intention* is to manipulate – otherwise it is just a learned courtesy, in just the same way that we learn other good manners we now practise without having to think. We were not born knowing we should say please and thank you; we had to learn, either by instruction or by following example.

Matching language and metaphor

Whilst the first stage of rapport-building is almost always behavioural, language quickly becomes important. Reflecting key words and metaphors – ideally using exactly the same words and terms as the other person – is a fast-track way to gain an even deeper rapport. The key is that we show we recognise and relate to *their* meaning and means of expressing it rather than translating it through our own systems of interpretation and expression. In essence, matching is the trick with spoken language just as much as it is with body language.

The pioneers of Neuro-Linguistic Programming (NLP) in the 1970s and 1980s recognised that individuals tend to rely more on one of the main sensory systems than others and that our language tends to reflect our broad preferences and habits in this area. For example, people who are inclined to do a lot of visualisation in their thinking favour visual words (*I see, that looks good, things are getting brighter . . .*). Those who think in words and *hear* the words reflect this in their speech (*that rings a bell, this sounds good . . .*). Those who think kinaesthetically are more likely to use metaphors drawn from physical experience (*I can't seem to get a grip on this, We need to move this on . . .*). There is a further NLP hypothesis that particular eye movements indicate in a reliable way what sensory system someone is using at any particular time but research on this is inconclusive. Rather than depending on the cues of specific eye movements, my practice is to pay attention to the overall patterns of speech that someone uses in determining their favoured sensory system.

This may seem like a nuance but it can be crucial. I remember once coaching a National Health Service chief executive and her chairman, having been brought in to help them resolve what they described as 'communication problems'. As we worked it became obvious to me that whereas the chief executive was largely visual in her language, the chairman's language was predominantly kinaesthetic. When I drew this to their attention and got them to practise reflecting back the exact language that they were hearing each other use, it built an essential bridge of understanding. They had almost literally been speaking different languages.

Building rapport with teams

It is relatively straightforward to create and maintain rapport with an individual – it is more complex with a team. I believe there are two rapport–building techniques that are particularly effective.

Match the team in terms of energy, pace and volume. Teams and groups tend to develop behavioural norms that can fluctuate during a day or a session. They have their moods and energy changes just as individuals do. At its simplest level, if I walk into a team meeting as a coach and perceive the group to be low in energy I need to engage with them at their level for a short period before attempting to raise the energy. It is a bit like fishing – if you strike too soon you will lose the fish. Nothing is as pointless and counter-productive as playing the 'dynamic coach' if your group is in an energy lull.

Pay attention to the body language of individuals within the group, and where necessary reflect it back with an aspect of your own body language. This is called cross-matching. For example, if when facilitating a session you need to engage in discussion with a particular team member you still need to pay attention to the body language of the rest of the group. Someone on the other side of the table who is fidgeting whilst you are occupied needs to know you are still connected with them. Moving a part of your body at the same pace and rhythm as the fidget – for example, twiddling the fingers of one hand in their direction – can be all that is needed. I would emphasise that this technique is one to use sparingly, otherwise you may end up looking like someone with multiple nervous tics!

Asking powerful questions

There are few aspects of leading and coaching teams that do not involve the need for a robust set of powerful, focused questions. The use of such questions overlaps each of the skill sets and, like rapport-building skills, is one of the absolute core skills that unites and binds the separate competencies.

The most powerful questions tend to be short and 'open', formulated in such a way that they offer the maximum stimulus to exploratory thought. Typically such questions will begin with either 'what . . . ?' or 'how . . .?'

When coaching one-to-one or facilitating it is useful to have a set of questions that can help establish the crux of an issue and provide a framework for exploring it and considering ways forward. Such a framework of questions should be used flexibly and with regard to the agenda at hand rather than in strict order for its own sake. The following list of questions can be applied, with discretion, to a very wide range of both individual and team issues:

- What is the core issue?
- How important is it on a 1–10 scale?
- Who has responsibility for this issue?
- How much motivation and energy to address it do you have – on the same 1–10 scale?
- What have you tried already?
- What have you learned from what you have tried?
- What similar issues have you faced in the past?
- What have you learned from these situations?
- What could be stopping you making progress on the issue?
- What might be the benefit you are getting from *not* addressing or solving it?
- What could be the consequences – short and longer term – of not addressing the issue?
- Focusing on you at your very best – what do you say to yourself about how to address this issue?
- What options do you have for action?
- How will you choose between these options?

- What is the next action to take?
- When will you take it?
- What support might you need?

There is no need to ask every question, and other questions can be useful too. The key is to develop a set of punchy, open questions that can guide you in helping a team – or individual – to think through those tougher issues that may not have obvious or immediate solutions. The team or individual does not even need to know you are following a structure – they just experience the benefits.

'Closed' questions – questions that tend to elicit a short or even one-word answer - are useful too, when used sparingly. They are best when used to reach a definite point in a coaching or facilitation session so that the session can move on; for example:

- Have you made a decision?
- Should we move on now?
- Have we spent enough time on this?
- Are you sufficiently clear?
- Does that feel right for you?

There is, however, no single formula for questioning that is guaranteed to produce consistent results. There is a preference in coaching and other helping disciplines for asking predominantly open questions, but this in itself is not going to produce consistent results. The sales research conducted by the Huthwaite organisation (Rackham, 1995) found that in a sales context sixty per cent of closed questions elicit an answer of longer than a sentence and ten per cent of open questions get a single word answer.

Questions to avoid

There are some types of question it is better to steer well clear of in a coaching or team coaching context. For example it is almost always better to avoid asking the question 'why?'. This may seem counter-intuitive, as the 'why' question seems such an obvious one to ask, but the fact is it is usually counter-productive. It is generally asked mainly to satisfy the curiosity of the questioner and tends to put the client on the defensive, requiring them to explain themselves. It is a useful question for journalists, politicians and scientists but not for coaches. The question 'Why haven't you solved this yet?' will have a very different impact from asking 'What is getting in the way of a solution here?'

Avoid 'advice in disguise' or loaded questions. Coaching and team coaching is a predominantly non-advisory function, but some questions by the way they are constructed can suggest what the coach thinks is best; for example,

'Don't you think it would be wise to confront your boss?' or 'Have you thought about giving your team mate some feedback?'.

Finally, avoid double or multiple questions. These only have the effect of confusing your client or team. The multiple, loaded 'why?' questions are best left to the likes of Jeremy Paxman and John Humphries who ask questions in the spirit of gladiatorial debate. This is not the role of the coach.

The skill set as it relates to other disciplines

One way of describing the skill of the team coach is to divide the key competencies into four main areas as follows:

1   One-to-one coaching skills as used in executive/business coaching
2   Facilitation skills for groups of all sizes
3   Team-building and training skills
4   Process consulting skills

Some may argue that in other contexts these skill sets can be seen as subsets of each other and this can indeed be the case. For example, someone acting as a consultant needs facilitation skills, a facilitator needs to be able to ask the powerful coaching questions associated with executive coaching and so on. My view would be that the team coach and the leader using a coaching style need aspects of all these skills if they are to operate effectively.

This is a broad skill set. The challenge for the team coach is to draw on each of these areas as appropriate and mix, match, blend and borrow as the situation demands.

Skills and knowledge drawn from one-to-one coaching

The emergence of one-to-one coaching as a tool for managers and leaders has been arguably the biggest success story in the past 20 years of management development activity. Reliable surveys, such as those conducted annually in the UK by the Chartered Institute of Personal Development (CIPD), point to an ascendant position for coaching as regards perceptions of effectiveness and return on investment.

Key aspects of the one-to-one coach's skill set have direct relevance for the team coach.

The one-to-one coach is variously referred to in organisational life as an executive coach, business coach or performance coach. He or she works to enable 'coachees' or clients to make progress on issues of their own choosing, primarily by use of active listening, summarising and asking highly focused questions. This general approach has spawned an impressive trail of innovative additional techniques and methodologies. There is general accord amongst coaching professionals that the role is primarily non-directive and non-advisory in nature – a structured conversation aimed at helping the client to identify his or her own way forward and means of getting there. The agenda for this kind of coaching is created by pressure to change, either generated by the personal and professional needs of the client or by a new demand or direction set by their organisation – or indeed by the combination of internal and external pressures. For example, an executive considering their career development during a coaching session may need to consider both the performance demands placed upon them by their organisation and weigh these against their changing personal perspective as they grow older.

As the coaching market has grown and matured there is now a mixed economy of coaching provision. Approaches vary from the use of external independent coaches who work primarily with the most senior staff, through to in-house coaches who have been trained to coach as part of their jobs but who tend not to have coaching as their sole function. There is also a strong rising trend for managers to be trained in a basic coaching approach as part of their skill set.

One-to-one coaches work on a wide range of issues. There are questions of career development, including identifying a trajectory, choosing a new job or developing new skills or qualifications. Relationship issues occur frequently, such as managing the boss, a colleague, a customer or client. Other typical subjects include dilemmas over how to respond to an immediate situation or solve a specific problem as well as more general issues of confidence, personal impact or presentation.

Coaches work with *process* rather than content. A key characteristic of coaching as opposed to other kinds of intervention for individuals such as mentoring is that the coach needs no expertise in any specific subject matter – they do not need to be experts in a particular industry or sector. Instead they work purely with process – that is, with the thinking, feeling and behavioural aspects of their clients.

Coaching can be truly transformational. It frequently involves the deeper aspects of an individual's being – feelings, beliefs and values – and this is one of the reasons it is so potent in effecting change: it is able to get beyond presenting symptomatic issues and get to the root or heart of what needs to happen to effect change.

The core skill set of the one-to-one coach contains the following abilities:

- To create and maintain rapport with the client
- To engage in an active partnership committed to the goals and process of coaching

- To listen actively
- To identify appropriate agenda items for coaching and create compelling goals for progress
- To help a client to generate new options for choice
- To help a client identify and deal with potential blockages to progress
- To offer clear feedback when necessary
- To work towards real actions and changes

Developing your one-to-one coaching skills

Coaching is a structured activity that has key disciplines and requires a specific set of attitudes and assumptions about how people learn and develop. You may already have many of the skills and personal attributes needed, but training is also essential. There are some useful organisations referred to in Chapter 8. A good working knowledge of what is involved can be gained from reading some of the excellent books on the market and in this area I would strongly recommend *Coaching Skills: A Handbook* (second edition) by Jenny Rogers (Rogers, 2008). But I would emphasise that nothing beats the practical skill and knowledge-building that a proper training and – subsequent supervision – can bring.

Theory related to one-to-one coaching

In addition to foundation skills training it is important to understand something of the underpinning psychological models that inform coaching theory and practice. Even a good training will offer only a broad introduction to these areas of knowledge. Practice really leads theory in coaching – it is successful precisely because it has direct practical value. Nonetheless, some understanding of the root theories on which coaching is based will substantially enrich the depth and scope of your coaching practice. Useful models include:

- Psychodynamic theories built on the works of pioneers such as Freud and Jung, including Gestalt (Perls, 1969) and Transactional Analysis (Berne, 1975).
- 'Person-centred' theories of personal development and counselling practice such as those of Carl Rogers (Rogers, 1961).
- Neuro Linguistic Programming (NLP) – a system of thinking that has drawn on the study of the structures of excellence in a variety of fields, critically in the area of communication, to spawn a range of genuinely radical and creative coaching techniques (Bandler, 1985).
- Knowledge of personality theories and their attendant psychometric instruments such as the MBTI (Briggs Myers, 1995) and the FIRO-B (Waterman and Rogers, 1996) – both world-class instruments that require training and licensing in their use, and which provide valuable

background theory, even for a coach who does not plan to use them directly in coaching.
- The 'Inner Game' model which Tim Gallwey developed as a ground-breaking approach to sports coaching (Gallwey, 1986) and later extended to the workplace (Gallwey, 1997).

One-to-one skills and team coaching

The similarities between the roles of one-to-one coach and team coach are that they both emphasise the need for good rapport, listening, summarising and questioning skills. Additionally they both assume a fundamental resourceful-ness on the part of the client or team member, what may be described as a 'change agenda'. Crucially, neither team coaching nor executive one-to-one coaching requires specific sector knowledge on the part of the coach – it is all about managing the process.

However, there are also some key differences between the roles. The team coach will act explicitly as a conduit to resources outside the team and therefore is likely to introduce relevant theories, techniques, exercises, tools or other resources which may help the team to learn or develop. The team coach has responsibilities to create structured events and meetings that are by their nature more complex than one-to-one coaching sessions. There are sub-tle interpersonal, psychological, structural and political dynamics to take into account in team coaching. Equivalent dynamics will affect the individual client in his or her working life, but they will not be literally present in the room. More individual feelings and thoughts within the team will remain hidden: if it is true that in individual coaching the client tends to hold some things back, it is even more likely in team coaching where individual members are gener-ally less likely to divulge information about which they may feel sensitive.

One-to-one coaching skills are most relevant in leading and coaching teams when individual members of the team need some personal attention and support in working their way through a particular issue or circumstance. They are also useful when the team needs the stimulus and challenge of powerful, focused questioning to help them deal with an issue, or when a team is bogged down in 'problem' mode and needs someone to help re-focus them on outcomes and goals. Finally they can be useful in providing a structured process of questioning that can take a team from defining an issue they need to work on, right through to identifying appropriate action.

Skills and knowledge drawn from facilitation practice

Facilitation has grown in importance as fewer decisions in organisations are made by diktat. Cooperative work within and between teams – even between organisations – has become ever more essential, and facilitation has proved its worth as a means of involving people in decision-making, as well as helping to foster positive relationships amongst – and between – teams.

The facilitator, like the coach, helps a team to attend to their *process* – to develop their strength, sense of purpose and confidence and improve not only their work but their *capacity* to work. Having the confidence as a facilitator to trust your process skills can take time. I remember vividly, many years ago, spending a day facilitating a team involved in highly technical work, when I had virtually no clue what they were talking about from start to finish – yet the day was deemed a great success and my skills seen as essential to that success. I focused my attention on the flow of the discussion, the changes in energy associated with the flow, and the fluctuating dynamics among members of the group. This, combined with a clear contracting process about what had to be achieved and by when, gave me a mandate to make interventions, interrupt when it seemed conversation was becoming circular or unfocused, give feedback and steer the discussion back to its essentials.

Detachment and impartiality

There is always a political dimension to organisational life. To have credibility, the facilitator needs to be aware of this dimension, yet immune to it. He or she must be disinterested about the outcome of a particular discussion. Any suspicion of bias will automatically make at least part of the group defensive and will probably cause them to question the integrity of both the facilitator and the process. This can complicate the role and sometimes even neutralise the value of the internal organisational facilitator.

For this reason, external specialist facilitators are particularly valuable in situations where representatives of separate organisations need to speak together and need facilitative help that is pristine in regard to perceived neutrality.

This neutral stance as regards outcomes is a crucial aspect of the team coaching role, but it does not follow that the team coach should be frigidly detached and without emotion as a person. It is my experience that a degree of warmth and friendliness in relationships with a team is very important, especially if you have to be 'tough', such as when offering challenging or sensitive feedback.

Issues facilitation can address

Facilitators work on a wide range of issues, typically including:

- Strategic discussions where senior teams need to debate future direction, strategy and policy

- Off-site meetings or away days where teams may meet to review progress, discuss future work and learn together
- Focus groups convened to discuss and analyse specific organisational issues
- Creative sessions aimed at generating new ideas for products or services

Additionally, facilitation skills may be useful in other types of meeting, including training and learning sessions – anything in fact where a neutral stance coupled with expertise in group process is relevant.

The facilitator's skill set

The core skill set of the facilitator overlaps considerably with that of the coach and consists of the following abilities:

- To create rapport simultaneously with a wide variety of people
- To create working partnerships and an agreed approach to working and learning – a contract of behaviour
- To structure events for maximum effect
- To record information
- To listen actively
- To hold a group to its agenda – usually by maintaining focus on one topic or issue at a time whilst keeping on track with the bigger picture and overall goals for a session
- To ask powerful questions that focus the group on core issues
- To deal with challenging behaviour – itself an art that requires a wide range of skills, including the ability to challenge back if necessary
- To succinctly summarise what you have heard
- To review the process
- To manage the discussion in terms of flow and energy so that the task is completed on time
- To observe and offer feedback, letting the group know what you are seeing and hearing

Developing your facilitation skills

As with coaching it is important to acquire a structured basic knowledge that provides a foundation to your facilitation skills, and there is no short cut to this – training is required. There are numerous providers of facilitation skills training. One reputable provider is the Chartered Institute of Personnel Development (CIPD) who can be found at www.cipd.co.uk. They provide both basic and advanced courses.

Skills drawn from team building practice

In 1980, whilst I was in my early social work career, a team leadership trainer introduced me to John Adair's Action Centred Leadership Theory and I experienced the first flash of illumination around team development. He drew the famous three-circle diagram (see Figure 2.1) and pointed out that the team leader needs to attend to each of three areas of team performance – task, team and individual – if a team is to perform and flourish (Adair, 1973). This model has inspired and informed many team-building events and leadership programmes and remains a robust and useful concept.

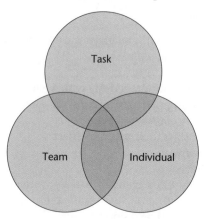

Figure 2.1 Adair's Action Centred Leadership model

Team coaching as an approach has been strongly informed by team-building exercises of the sort that have been developed particularly in the USA and the UK over several decades. The team-building approach can be traced back to 1920s America, when the first experiments connecting the idea of team morale to performance were conducted by Elton Mayo, who became known as the 'father' of the Human Relations Movement. Mayo conducted his experiments in the Hawthorne organisation, and concluded that the most important improvements in worker morale and productivity could be achieved by creating positive group dynamics and a sense of group belonging (Mayo, 1933).

Theory related to team-building

Since these early studies, research on team effectiveness has grown, drawing from diverse academic fields. These include particularly influential studies by:

- Kurt Lewin, founder of the Center for Research in Group Dynamics, who emphasised the prime importance of leadership behaviour on team effectiveness (Lewin and Lippitt, 1938).
- Douglas McGregor, who explored the implications of polarised assumptions around what motivated workers to better performance, contrasting the theory X approach that emphasised command and control with the more empowering theory Y leadership style (McGregor, 2006).
- Meredith Belbin, who looked at the importance of distinct roles taken by individuals in developing highly effective teams – a move away from the implicit idea that top teams were to be created by putting lots of very clever people together (Belbin, 1981).
- Abraham Maslow, who formulated an influential theory on motivational factors at work, in which social belonging and recognition – such as that to be had in teams – forms a key part (Maslow, 1987).
- Bruce Tuckman, who described the developmental stages teams must go through if they are to reach a high performing stage – the well-known forming/storming/norming/performing/adjourning model (Tuckman, 1965).
- John Adair, who identified the key areas that leaders needed to concern themselves with – specifically how to achieve a given task, build and motivate teams and support individuals – and was an advocate of team-building exercises (Adair, 1973).
- Isabel Briggs Myers and Katharine Cook Briggs, who drew on Jung's work on psychological types (Jung, 1991) to develop the Myers-Briggs Type Inventory (MBTI). In team development terms their contribution has been to emphasise the need to understand, value and use the different personality types in teams (Briggs Myers, 1995).

These models were developed largely between the 1940s and the 1980s but their influence remains strong. Each has attracted criticism and each has undergone at least partial revision over time, but together they have formed a bedrock of ideas on which other theories and models have grown and in which much team-building practice has been grounded.

In the UK and the USA interest in the team rather than the individual as the prime unit of organisational performance has accelerated since the 1970s and 1980s, spawning a host of team-building companies, in-house team development specialists and individual trainers and consultants who specialise in team-building.

How do team-building events work?

The typical team-building event lasts one or two days and is designed to stand alone. They are usually held off-site, sometimes at well-equipped specialist centres, sometimes at hotels or conference centres. They have a general orientation towards 'experiential' learning – active learning based on teams participating in one or more time-limited tasks aimed at exploring team effectiveness across a number of dimensions, including communication, support, planning and other working processes. Many follow a process loosely based on the Kolb Learning Cycle, which has been modified and described in varying terms, but which in essence involves learning through a combination of direct experience, reflection, forming abstract concepts or hypotheses, and trying the learning thus generated in new circumstances (Kolb and Fry, 1975). Some organisations simplify this learning process into brief operating slogans such as: *do, review, apply*.

A typical sequence of events at such a team-building course might run as follows:

- The trainer introduces a practical problem-solving task, usually time-limited.
- The team sets about the task.
- The trainer reviews the task with the team, highlighting areas of team functioning such as leadership, communication, planning, use of resources and creativity.
- The review is reinforced by relevant theoretical inputs.
- The team is invited to think about how the learning from the process can be applied back at work.

The main attraction and benefit of these kinds of events is drawn from their *intensity* and *immediacy*. Behaviour during exercises and problem-solving activities is seen to have immediate consequences or effects – in the public context of the whole team working together. Additionally, feedback can follow quickly from activity to activity. Activities can be selected to address direct issues drawn from review and discussion, thus guaranteeing their perceived relevance to real team issues. There is a 'whole person' dimension – people get involved physically, intellectually and emotionally – and when events are held in spectacular countryside settings there is often a real connection with the metaphor of outdoor challenge for many team members. Levels of challenge and support can be regulated quickly and with wide parameters; some teams relish very high challenge, others need a more supportive approach. Of critical significance is the fact it is usually easy to see how individual or group behaviour during an exercise parallels or reflects behaviour back in the work place. It does seem as if individuals approach games in much the same way they approach work. Finally, planning for real change back in the work place can follow directly from high-impact direct learning experience – the reason to make changes can become crystal clear.

As with all team development activities, good design, facilitation and management are of paramount importance. The main dangers of getting things wrong are:

- Pandering to an influential leader or sub-group within a team who may favour a particular form of activity or style of event that may not suit the needs of the wider team
- Offering too much in the way of physical activities that put individual group members at a disadvantage due to issues of fitness or health
- Offering too high a level of challenge that can put individuals or even a whole team into a 'panic' rather than a 'stretch' zone
- Failing to recognise cultural issues that have a bearing on the style of event or exercise that works well for everyone
- Losing connection with learning goals in the interests of offering vivid experiences for their own sake

It is also important to build flexibility into a programme. These are by nature dynamic learning events and as the team learns it may be necessary to change emphasis or introduce different elements into a programme to reflect new learning needs.

Skills and knowledge drawn from process consulting

The term 'consultant' conveys a number of different meanings and evokes a variety of responses, often rather negative. I remember once being asked by a London taxi driver what I did for a living. When I said I was a management consultant he sighed heavily and shut the window, saying not another word until the end of the journey. In many organisations with which I have worked the word 'consultant' evokes similar reactions of cynicism and contempt. They are often perceived as overpaid charlatans who take a long time to tell you what you already know, at enormous expense, and whose recommendations are frequently not accepted by the client organisation because they do not take into account their particular circumstances.

But there are a number of different models of consultancy, each operating in distinctly different ways. One way of differentiating between them is to consider a spectrum that moves from *guru*, through *doctor/patient* to *process consultant*. The 'guru' model of consultant is regarded as an authority on his or her subject, essentially hired for their expertise in a given area. An example might be where an organisation needs to implement a new accounting or HR system and does not have the resources or expertise to do so. The 'guru' consultant will be hired to provide recommendations and processes based on their expert knowledge.

The 'doctor/patient' model describes a situation where an organisation detects that something is wrong and calls in a consultant who will both diagnose the problem and prescribe a solution. Their success depends on creating a sufficient level of trust with the parts of the organisation thought to be 'sick' to get accurate information from them in order to create a realistic diagnosis.

Both these models are dependent for their success on the organisation being prepared to accept the solution described by the consultant. In both, the organisation or people within it are essentially recipients of a service. There is considerable evidence that both these kinds of consulting model have limited effectiveness unless their intervention is very skilfully managed by the client organisation.

The process consultant in contrast works in a contracted partnership arrangement with the following broad assumptions:

- Clients need help to discover what their issue or problem really is.
- Clients do not necessarily know what kind of help they need.
- Clients want to improve things but need help in defining what they need to improve and how to do it.
- Most organisations can be helped to diagnose their own situations, strengths and weaknesses.
- The client will always know more about the organisation than the consultant can ever hope to learn and this knowledge needs to be drawn upon.
- The client ultimately needs to think through both issues and solutions themselves if they are to fully commit to a plan of action.
- The process consultant will build the clients own skills in understanding and dealing with organisational issues – essentially, teach them how to fish rather than just give them a fish.

These principles are drawn from the work of Edgar Schein who went on to define process consulting as 'a set of activities on the part of the consultant that help the client to perceive, understand and act upon the process events that occur in the client's environment in order to improve the situation as defined by the client' (Schein, 1988).

This model has close parallels with the principles that underpin most non-advisory forms of one-to-one executive coaching:

- Coaching is about closing the gap between potential and performance individually and organisationally.
- Coaching is about change and action. It provides the opportunity for a conversation of unique frankness which contains the high support and high challenge that will move the client to greater effectiveness.

- Clients are resourceful people: they do not need to be 'fixed', pandered to or 'cured'.
- The coach's role is to work with the client so they can answer their own questions. A good coach has searching questions, not advice or generic solutions.
- For the purpose of coaching, the coach and client are equals; it is an adult-adult partnership.
- Coaching at work is about performance at work. However, the whole-person perspective will deepen and extend the range of what the skilled coach can achieve with the client.

As with coaching, the process consultant will be long on listening and skilled questioning and short on advice.

Process consulting is often pictured as a cycle (see Figure 2.2). A typical team coaching assignment would follow at least the early stages. These stages – gaining entry, contracting, gathering data and feeding back the data – will typically involve the team leader, individual members of the team and, often, external stakeholders or even customers. The latter stages will typically involve the whole team but will be mixed with other kinds of activity and process.

Gaining entry is fundamentally about establishing rapport and credibility and indicating a suitability to engage with the team. This is a key area for demonstrating listening skills and displaying personal integrity, openness and

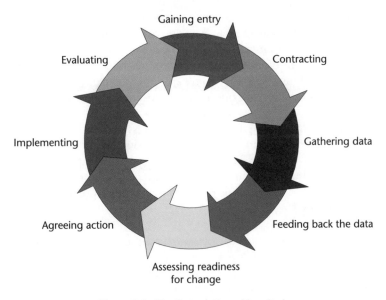

Figure 2.2 The Process Consulting Cycle

trustworthiness. The client is often nervous about the whole process and will be highly sensitive to any negative behaviours or signs the coach may give out.

Contracting is the process of agreeing expectations about the work. These vary from formal expectations such as how much work is expected, fees and key outputs, right through to less formal but vital expectations about behaviour, responsibilities and attitudes. It is likely that a team coach will have to contract first with a team leader and then with the team. Part of this 'whole team' contracting will be about reassuring the team that you are there to act in the interests of everyone and are not the leader's 'lackey'– this is absolutely vital if the team is to believe in you, no matter how highly they regard their leader.

In team coaching the process begins to expand beyond the parameters of the consulting cycle after these initial stages to include some of the wide variety of activities described elsewhere in this chapter.

Summary

Just like one-to-one coaching, team coaching can get rather messy. There are occasions where the theories don't seem to apply and the techniques don't work. Indeed, largely due to the sheer dynamics of working with greater numbers it is likely that the team coaching scenario will reveal more complexities, uncertainties and even mysteries than one-to-one coaching is likely to throw up. This can begin even before the diagnostic process: as soon as a mooted team development process is in the wind individuals will be responding to the prospect in a variety of ways based on personality, politics and sometimes interest in some kind of personal advantage. There is always an element of individual emotional response to the idea of team development and these responses can vary widely. Personal agendas can be extremely important but will often remain unspoken. Individuals can be:

- Excited – 'At last we'll make some progress.'
- Scared – 'Will so and so try and make a fool of me?'
- Sceptical – even cynical – 'It's just a load of management bxxxxxxs.'
- Wary – 'I hope there are no stupid games or naval-gazing.'
- Frustrated – 'Don't people realise I've got a job to do? There's no time for all this.'

Team leaders can often fear being exposed by these exercises and in addition may fear losing a degree of control or influence to the coach. It is therefore important to reassure and to acknowledge strengths as well as to offer challenges. Human nature can prove to be the dominant factor and it is important to remind yourself that this is 'not a game of perfect'.

Key learning points

- Team coaching requires a complex skill set, but happily many of the skills overlap.
- Rapport building skills are absolutely essential.
- A set of powerful questions, learned by heart, is also essential.
- A good contracting agreement will provide an anchor for managing behaviour and process and should be conducted thoroughly even with a willing and able team.
- Remaining neutral and disinterested is vital if you are to build and retain trust and credibility with the team.

Reflective questions

- Where are you strongest in your skill set and what would you most need to develop?
- What are your emotional needs in a team coaching environment? Do you have the right mix of detachment from specific outcomes and commitment to a process focus?
- What areas of theory and background knowledge do you most need to investigate?

3 The coaching approach to leading teams

A leader is part of the team, and is an integral, indeed critical part of it in terms of its dynamic and working effectiveness. Because of this the leader can never have the detached perspective of the external coach and can never operate entirely free from a personal viewpoint. Nonetheless, much of the knowledge and skill that a team coach should possess can be invaluable for the leader in terms of understanding where their team is in terms of effectiveness and in being able to offer models and templates to map its growth. Similarly the leader can benefit from learning the personal and interpersonal skills needed to deal flexibly and purposefully with the many challenges that leading a team can present. Team coaching methodology can offer the leader numerous practical tools to help a team overcome its weaknesses and build on its strengths.

Taking a coaching role as a leader is challenging. It requires high emotional intelligence, behavioural flexibility, humility and a willingness to trust the team enough to make them responsible for performance on which the leader will be judged. In addition the leader needs the judgement to know when a coaching style is the best one to use, and the clarity of communication to let the team know clearly when he or she is in coaching mode and when not. Coaching is not for every leadership situation but is best used when the team as a whole needs to exercise ownership and responsibility for a given situation.

Using a coaching approach as a team leader means, amongst other things:

- Taking a facilitative role in some team discussions – for example, where the team is looking for fresh ideas
- Asking good questions for the team to work on rather than offering all the answers
- Listening more than talking
- Working to establish 'stretch' goals for the team
- Devolving tasks and delegating responsibility as far as is practicable
- Abandoning 'boss-iness' as a personal style and adopting an adult-adult collegiate approach as far as possible

The essential factor is adopting a coaching mindset – a mindset that says the leader is not there to control, manipulate or outshine but to draw out the full potential of the team and get performance from them. This is something that is often intellectually acceptable to leaders but their instincts or personalities may inhibit them from committing to the style; their ingrained beliefs and anxiety about losing control may make the challenge feel too great. Such leaders will need strong evidence that a coaching style can be beneficial. This chapter aims to offer evidence that it can.

Specific areas where a leader can use coaching skills

- In creative or brainstorming sessions where the team is looking for new ideas
- Where the team is looking to review its functioning with a view to learning and developing capability
- When the team is engaged in strategic thinking and planning
- When the team is faced with new circumstances and has to make changes
- When individuals in the team need specific attention or support and the team can help
- When there is conflict that needs to be understood and worked through in a positive way
- When challenging the team to raise its game

Key aspects of the 'leader as coach' role

When a team leader uses a coaching style the dynamics are significantly different from when a team works with an external coach. The main practical differences between the leader who takes a coaching approach and the specialist team coach can be summarised as follows:

Leaders who use coaching skills	Specialist team coach
Are with or around the team for most or much of the time	Will usually only see the team at intervals
Will spend considerable time with individuals in the team	Will tend to speak to individuals in the team only sporadically
Will have history with the team, probably including some conflict or having had to make unpopular decisions	Will know only a part of the history of the team and its interpersonal relationships at work

Leaders who use coaching skills	Specialist team coach
Will work intensely with the team at work itself and will not have a wholly neutral viewpoint	Will normally see the team only at specially convened occasions, unless observing meetings or shadowing a member of the team. Will maintain a neutral stance
Holds direct accountability and authority for the team's performance	Is not directly accountable for the team's performance and holds no positional authority

How leaders can coach their teams in practice

The first requirement for the leader who wants to take a coaching approach is to understand that they are there to get results from other people rather than knowing it all or doing it all themselves. This can be an uncomfortable challenge for even the best team leaders and I have seen very few who manage it well. I have seen broadly talented, well-meaning team leaders who oscillate between a coaching and a telling style without warning or clear signalling, leading to confusion amongst the team. Others may ask their teams to take ownership of an important issue but make it clear through their words and body language the answer they really want to hear. Some appear to abdicate responsibility by being completely hands off rather than acting as a leader who is choosing a coaching style. Still others say they are coaching but are really mentoring, in the sense of offering their advice and experience.

Keys to using a successful coaching style as a team leader

Develop a clear method of signalling to your team what mode you are operating in – for example, let them know when you are facilitating rather than persuading or advocating. Get into the habit when you ask the team a question of listening to everyone else before you say what you think, in order not to over-influence their responses. Once you have made your position clear it can be hard for the team members to offer a contradictory view. Ensure you discuss your role as leader within the team, including when and how a coaching style can be appropriate and effective. It can be useful to devise a simple contracting protocol for clarifying expectations on the behaviours you will use. It will be hugely beneficial to develop real familiarity and ease with the powerful questions discussed in Chapter 2 – these are a durable and potent part of the coach's tool kit.

The team leader as coach can also adopt a coaching style in working one-to-one with individual members of the team (see Chapter 2 for a description of one-to-one coaching).

The importance of trust for the leader

From direct experience of working in and with teams I can say with confidence that the leader's level of trustworthiness is certainly one of the absolute keys to successful team leadership. I have never come across a really high-performing team where trust for the leader is low. The leader has the critical role in setting a climate where trust can flourish. A number of research models corroborate this view. For example, the Johari Window model emphasises the importance of openness in effective communication (Luft, 1969). Specifically, being able to listen to feedback about oneself and to disclose in a frank way one's views, opinions and feelings is a key to building positive and trustworthy communications. The Johari window model makes a direct connection between open disclosure, readiness to receive feedback and a close correlation between how others see you and how you see yourself. The closer people are to seeing the 'real' you the more likely they are to trust you. There is a full explanation of the model at the www.businessballs.com website.

Believing in the team

Mindset and attitude are at least as important as skill in this role. When coaching from a position of leadership you will need to operate under the assumption that you are there largely to get performance out of others. If you are to use a coaching style effectively, you need to believe in the resourcefulness of the team – and transmit your belief in that resourcefulness – even when finding some of the behaviours of the team challenging or frustrating. This is not just an abstract requirement but a crucial aspect of successfully employing a coaching style as a leader. A belief in the resourcefulness of others is not an intellectual proposition – ultimately it is not intellectually provable – but is an underpinning assumption that creates impact on everything we do and say in a leading or a coaching role.

Research on what people believe others expect of them shows that core expectations are set very early on in a relationship – and much of the expectation is set not so much in terms of *what* is said but *how* it is said in terms of body language and voice tone. You might cast your mind back to when you were at school and a new teacher walked into the classroom: how long did it take you to weigh up what they expected of the pupils in terms of their behaviour? When I ask this question in groups I train, the majority of people say that they knew where they stood with a new teacher in as little as ten seconds. Leaders have the same kind of impact: if your body language and tone convey the impression that you do not expect the team and its members to perform well, little that you say will make much positive difference.

You have to believe in your bones that the team can succeed if you are to lead them to success – even if you may have to work hard in coaching and developing them to draw out their potential. If you really believe your team are no-hopers then it may be time to look for another job or to get some new team members.

When not to use a coaching style

A coaching approach on the part of the leader can be especially effective when working with teams that are performing well in one or more aspects of their functioning – but this does not mean it is the right approach for every circumstance. It would usually be inappropriate to use a predominantly coaching style when:

- The team lacks basic competence or experience and needs more guidance in getting to the first base of capability.
- The team is still in a forming stage and is looking to the leader to set a tone rather than coach.
- The leader has specialist expertise to offer over a specific issue.
- Operational or strategic imperatives require a more hands on or directive approach.
- The team is clearly asking to be led rather than be coached when the leader has experience to offer in specific circumstances.

The 'Team Climate' model – a framework for success

This is one of the best theoretical frameworks for team leadership – and is also extremely useful for the team coach. It uses the metaphor of 'climate' as a way of describing the psychological and emotional conditions under which a team operates – conditions which are highly influenced by the leader. There is considerable depth of research that demonstrates how a team can flourish when the leader sets the right kind of climate. The original research was undertaken by Kurt Lewin, a German Jew who fled Germany in the 1930s. He ran action research exercises in which groups were led in different ways and leadership style was the only variable in how the groups were selected and treated (Lewin and Lippitt, 1938). This research was continued in the 1960s by George Litwin and Robert Stringer (Litwin and Stringer, 1969). They compared the effect of three basic leadership styles on both team performance and morale. The three styles were:

Authoritarian – A stern, autocratic style emphasising rules, conformity and essentially negative feedback. This style was demonstrated to create the following consistent results:

- High initial productivity
- Subversive behaviour breaking out amongst the team with covert or overt struggles for power with the leader
- Inability to innovate or use flexible working methods
- Inability to keep costs competitive
- Lower overall productivity
- A gradual decline in interest in the quality of the work done
- A conservative, formal and emotionally 'cold' team climate, sometimes with bullying or scapegoating

In my experience as a team coach I have encountered relatively few teams led in an unalloyed authoritarian style but have come across numerous teams where this is the basic underpinning model. Specifically I remember a manufacturing company run on these lines where the following features and behaviours were in evidence:

- Rigid insistence on rules, including a clock-in system and financial penalties for any lateness
- Strict insistence on conformity to the 'way things were done' and no tolerance of experimentation or creativity
- A sullen 'couldn't care less' air on the part of the workers, who were known to sabotage the heavy machinery if they felt like an extended break, and who would do as little as possible for as long as they were not directly supervised
- Tense relationships between authority figures – managers and foremen – and the workers
- The existence of bullying cliques amongst the workers who would intimidate new staff and connive to get the softest work for themselves

In such cultures there is often an assumption on the part of the leaders that the authoritarian style represents simple common sense – that anything else is inevitably 'soft' or even 'new-agey'. One common result of such a style is the low level of trust that is created between leader and teams – without which there is *never* a high level of loyalty and commitment. Critically, it becomes extremely hard for teams – and organisations – led in such a way to adapt to changes in their operating circumstances with changes in the way they work. Team members can become belligerent, entrenched and unwilling to adapt or take on new responsibilities. Many of the industries that suffered from strikes and industrial action in the UK of the late 1960s, 1970s and early 1980s were led in this fashion.

Laissez-faire – A leadership style focused on emotional support, co-operative behaviour, consensus decision-making and relationship-building – but with little in the way of goal-focus or direction. This style was demonstrated to produce the following consistent results:

- An initially pleasant working climate
- Low focus high performance
- Low productivity
- Growing frustration caused by lack of achievement and progress
- Increasing interpersonal tension, including the formation of cliques and pair-bonding
- Explicit or hidden struggles for leadership

I have worked with – and indeed in – a number of teams led this way. I remember one particular team I worked with that consisted of senior local authority managers. We decided at one stage we would engage in an outdoor-based development exercise aimed at enhancing mutual understanding and appreciation and boosting the team's problem-solving capabilities. I led the team through a structured sequence of problem-solving exercises over two days. The team attempted each exercise willingly but struggled to succeed in solving the challenges or problems set. This did not seem to concern them unduly and they remained apparently cheerful. At the end of the second day we were reviewing the programme and I asked the team a simple open question along the lines of 'How do you think you are doing so far?' The response was unanimous – everyone thought they were doing very well indeed. Intrigued, I asked them why they thought this to be the case, and they answered that they had completed two days without arguing – something they were pleased to have achieved and which they believed demonstrated positive team working. I pointed out that they had failed to succeed in any of the tasks set. This perturbed them a little but they maintained that sustaining a 'positive' team outlook was their definition of success. I used this as an opportunity to introduce 'climate' theory and it was a real light-bulb moment for them. They recognised that their team behaviour was highly influenced by the prevailing council culture which was civilised but underpowered in terms of achievement. In further discussion they admitted they had to put in immense effort to maintain the civilised veneer of polite interpersonal behaviour and that there were in fact numerous interpersonal tensions and 'elephants in the room'. In fact they tended to experience high levels of personal stress even though they felt they were, if anything, under-employed in terms of volume and intensity of work.

We were able to go on to look at how they could move towards a more achievement-focused style (see below), beginning with an informal 'scoring' of how they currently assessed themselves against five key criteria associated team success. This marked the beginning of the team moving towards a much more purposeful and effective style of working.

The Achievement-Focused/Democratic style – a purposeful, organised style of leadership that concentrates on galvanising the energy and effort of the team towards achieving challenging goals and standards. This style was demonstrated to produce the following consistent results:

- High morale even though the team works very hard
- High standards of work
- High levels of productivity
- An ability to be flexible and creative
- A climate that supports constructive conflict when it is directed at improving standards

During the research into this model it became clear that it is the *leader* whose influence has by far the highest impact on the creation of this kind of successful team climate. The practical lesson for leaders is to focus on five key areas of team performance and behaviour, as follows:

- *Clarity* – ensuring that everyone is clear as to the overall purpose of the team: how they fit in, what their role is, what they are expected to contribute, what the team's values are and what this means for behaviour, how things are done, how decisions are made, and so on
- *Standards* – ensuring that these are set at the highest possible level, with an emphasis on encouraging team members to push for ever higher standards and goals. This includes clarity on the consequences of standards not being met.
- *Responsibility* – an emphasis on devolving responsibility to individuals as far as possible, giving them ownership, authority and accountability
- *Recognition* – creating a climate focused on positive reinforcement – 'catching people doing things right'. This also means finding explicit means of reward for high performance – not necessarily financial, or even formal reward, but, for example, public praise for achievement coupled with small token rewards.
- *Teamwork* – ensuring that adequate time and energy is invested in maintaining and improving *how* the team is working – for example, by regular team meetings, development events, opportunities to brainstorm ideas, reviews of progress, planning sessions and so on. In addition there is an emphasis on creating *pride* in the team – talking it up in other circles and backing each other up as colleagues in public.

Very recently I worked in a team within the National Health Service which exemplifies the type. Despite there being no more than one or two conspicuously able team members and despite being asked to work miracles with skeletal resources they produce consistently excellent services in a deprived and challenging social, political and financial context. They work ludicrously hard but seem to thrive on it for the main part. The leader is cheerful, funny and warm but brooks no nonsense and focuses relentlessly on the task in hand. She also reminds the team constantly of what they are trying to achieve and makes sure that no time is wasted on irrelevant issues. I have spoken privately to each of the team and they all feel they can trust her; they respect her and they feel both challenged and supported by her. Each one feels evident pride in their own work and that of the team and whilst they feel stretched they know that they will be supported if for any reason they find they cannot cope.

The 'Climate Lab' simulation

The research findings on climate theory formed the basis of a simulation called 'The Climate Lab', which was developed in a partnership between Management Futures Ltd and American consultant John Bray in the year 2000. (Initially this was available as a commercial package but sale has been discontinued as it is complex to run and needs confident, expert facilitation. Nonetheless I and my colleagues still use it regularly.)

The simulation works like this: a group of participants between nine and twenty-four in number is divided into three teams of roughly equal size. Each team is taken away to a working room where they are shown a piece of video, welcoming them to the simulation and describing the nature of the company they are to work for. The first team is called 'Synergy' and they are shown a short film of a pleasant-natured manager welcoming them to a company run on *laissez-faire* lines. The second team is shown a film featuring a purposeful, dynamic leader who welcomes them to a company called 'Top Flight', run on *achievement-focused/democratic* lines. The third team is welcomed by a film featuring a rather forbidding manager welcoming them to work with 'Precision', a firm modelled on the *authoritarian* model. None of the team members are told anything explicit at this stage about the style of the team they are in. The teams are told they are to compete to secure a notional government contract. Their work will be assessed and measured for quality and quantity and the winning team will be awarded the contract. The teams are set to work manufacturing complex model aircraft. The work is supervised by the team manager – played in the appropriate style for each particular team by a professional actor. After two hours the work stops. Each member of each team is given a questionnaire asking them to assess their experience against the five core criteria – clarity, standards, responsibility, recognition and teamwork. The results of the work are calculated and the scores from the questionnaires correlated. During a review session the experiences of each team are shared and compared and the results revealed. The results are startlingly consistent. Virtually without exception the 'Top Flight' achievement-focused team outperforms the others and reports much higher morale and motivation according to the terms of the questionnaire. The groups then undertake an exercise looking at how they can improve the 'climate' scores of teams they lead, in a practical planning session.

Other lessons and implications of Climate Theory

Continuing research has shown up the following additional benefits of leading a team in an *achievement-focused/democratic* style:

- A positive team climate can be achieved even when the surrounding organisational culture is sub-optimal or negative. I have seen this happen time and again in large organisations undergoing morale-sapping change and invariably it is the team leader's example and behaviour that is largely responsible.
- A positive team climate can be perceived almost immediately by those on the outside looking in, such as customers, other stakeholders or members of different parts of the same organisation. As an ordinary member of the public one only has to walk into a shop or restaurant to know how well managed it is – the attitudes and behaviours of the staff tell the story very quickly.
- A positive team leadership style can overcome almost all other factors such as personality mix or a lack of star performers. I have frequently been struck by the force of this when running the 'Climate Lab' simulation. No matter what kind of organisation is involved or how the teams are selected for the exercise – by random selection or by some form of deliberately engineered process – the outcomes in terms of behaviour and performance are amazingly consistent.

Key leadership behaviours that promote high performance in teams

It is ultimately a subjective matter to discuss the behaviour and personalities of individuals who seem to be successful in the team leadership role. I have encountered the quiet and the noisy, the big and the small and all kinds of frankly eccentric team leaders who have been gifted in the role. What research there is indicates that the key qualities are very 'human' in nature, as opposed to the abstract factors such as 'strategic thinking ability' one might assume to be important. Research over a ten year period by Kouzes and Posner canvassed views from all over the world as to the most valued qualities or characteristics to be (Kouzes and Posner, 1993). These were the top five: honest, forward looking, competent, inspiring, intelligent.

In the same research, the authors described the actual behaviours used by effective leaders, as described by the teams they lead, in these terms: The leader

Supported me	Had the courage to do the right thing
Challenged me	Acted as a mentor to others
Listened	Celebrated good work
Followed through on commitments	Trusted me
Empowered others	Made time for people
Shared the vision	Opened doors
Overcame personal hardship	Admitted mistakes
Advised others	Solved problems creatively
Taught well	

My personal list would include:

- Credibility – whether drawn from relevant experience, expertise, talent or knowledge
- Integrity – having a strong moral compass and authority
- Toughness and resilience – being able to manage their own stress and to be calm under pressure
- Vision – an ability to see the big picture and what is needed to be done over the longer term
- Charisma – an elusive concept but associated with a combination of authority and approachability
- Humour – particularly the ability to laugh at oneself

Real leaders who coach

I have had the opportunity over the years to work with numerous leaders of teams who frequently adopted a coaching style. They would do this in their own highly individual way, but one characteristic they shared was to treat their team with a high degree of respect – they believed in their teams and they expected them to perform at a high level. Some of these leaders may not have been aware they were using a coaching approach at the time, but instinctively believed in the resourcefulness of the team and acted to get the best out of them.

One example that comes to mind is a leader in the media whom I worked with for many years. He would habitually state an issue or problem that he wanted the team to engage with and would give them full authority to work out what they were going to do and to instigate action. He would confine himself to asking challenging questions of the team and would usually keep his own views for the end of a discussion, even then not usually seeking to assert himself. He even accepted delegation from the team when the team identified him as being the best person to do a particular task. His teams were always characterised by an almost ferocious energy and commitment. They would frequently argue amongst themselves – but, crucially, about what needed to be done rather than about each other.

Another leader, from the pharmaceutical sector, ran such an achievement-focused/democratic style of team that he was sometimes told his own contribution to a piece of work needed to improve! This may sound like a nightmare to a more conservative style of leader but his team respected him hugely and were passionate over-achievers with an astonishing camaraderie.

Of the leaders I have worked with who would use coaching skills at least some of the time, the most frequently occurring weakness of approach would be a tendency to move from one style of leadership to another without warning. This could have the effect of disorienting the team and making them wary. My contribution as a team coach, when working with leaders who did this, was to give them feedback on the impact of their behaviour and coach them in how to signal a change of mode more clearly.

Working as a team coach with an ineffective team leader

From time to time it becomes apparent in working with a team as a coach that it is the leader who is at the heart of a team's problems. This can be a critical 'moment of truth' for the team coach, for a number of ethical and emotional reasons: usually the leader is the first point of contact for the coach and is therefore the first person with whom the coach develops a working relationship. This can create tensions around loyalty. The leader is often the one who pays the bill or who authorises payment, and the team coach who handles the leader poorly might be sacked from the assignment. The leader can often fear losing control or authority to the coach, and if the coach has to confront him or her with negative feedback it can increase these fears, causing the leader to act defensively or negatively.

In short, if the leader is weak or ineffective in any way it poses some tricky political and practical issues for the team coach. There is a danger that the coach will collude with the leader's poor behaviour or performance thus alienating the rest of the team, or back off from tackling the leader due to fear of being rejected or dismissed. A further danger is that the coach may handle the situation clumsily in public thus further weakening the leader's credibility and with it the confidence of the team.

What is required in these circumstances from the team coach is tactful but firm negotiation with the leader from the outset to create the expectation that the coach is working for the whole team. It can also be useful to issue a form of public contract to this effect with the whole team (see the section on *contracting* in Chapter 2). Underlying these measures is the need for courage to confront the leader and offer skilful feedback, and for integrity to walk away if you feel you cannot realistically add value should the leader be undermining your efforts.

Summary

For a team leader, a coaching approach combined with an achievement-focused/democratic style is particularly powerful in creating high performance. It demands both character and competence. For any leader seeking to make an art of their work and realise their own full potential in the role, the coaching approach is the route to follow. The techniques, theories and methods described in this book are a helpful foundation for fulfilling this role; the commitment and vision of the individual leader are what is required to make them really work.

Key learning points

- Leaders need to be selective in using a coaching style – it is not effective in every team situation.
- Leaders need to signal clearly with their teams when they are using a coaching approach and when they are not.
- The team leader needs to generate a climate of trust where open communication is encouraged and supported if a coaching style is to be effective.
- The team leader needs to genuinely believe in the ability and potential of the team – and convey this belief.
- The team coach needs to contract clearly with the leader that they are there to work on behalf of the whole team.

Reflective questions

If you are the leader of a team:

- What is your personal mental model of leadership in relation to the three options described in the 'climate' research?
- How could you adapt your leadership approach to be closer to the Achievement-Focused/Democratic style?
- How could you benefit from taking more of a coaching approach with your team?
- How trustworthy does your team really think you are? And how much do you believe in them and their ability to perform?

4 The challenge of the high performing team

Leadership as a topic seems to fascinate people. Every bookshop has scores of books on the subject. The newspapers are constantly dwelling on the perceived merits – and more often de-merits – of leaders in all walks of life, from commerce to government to sport. Most big organisations direct substantial amounts of energy and money at developing leadership capacity. Some organisations attempt to make a science of the subject, painstakingly creating laborious and unwieldy competency frameworks as some kind of assurance that leadership will flourish – yet at the same time give their leaders impossible tasks and non-stop negative feedback.

Research findings and theoretical frameworks approach the subject from a bewildering number of perspectives, leaving the student of leadership overwhelmed. Is there an ideal set of competencies? Is the elusive concept of 'character' more important? Is there an ideal set of behaviours? Or values? Just what is this thing called 'vision'? What should the ideal leader focus on – strategy, problem-solving, learning or people development? The essence of leadership seems elusive – yet we know it when we see it and, if not, we feel its absence.

There is a lot of attention on leadership involving crisis management or problem solving – turning round failing situations or dealing with emergencies. Relatively neglected are the challenges associated with leading teams that are seen as high performing.

Facing the challenge

Leading and coaching high performing teams can be an exhilarating privilege – and every bit as challenging as working with teams in need of urgent, even remedial interventions. Some of these challenges may not be immediately apparent. If you are the leader of a high performing team, you might ask yourself, can you:

- Stay out of the way and let others do what they are good at without interference?
- Stand back and let others excel and take the credit?
- Trust the team to handle matters for which you are ultimately accountable?
- Live with the fact that when teams are successful their high performance is likely to be taken for granted and praise may not come your way?
- Accept the fact that luck may have a part to play, since some potentially successful teams are asked to do jobs that are simply not 'do-able' due to organisational pressure whereas others have a relatively easy ride?
- Accept the fact that when a failure *does* occur you are likely to shoulder the blame?

For the team coach there are similar challenges in working with successful teams. However, unlike the role of leader there is far less discussion and theorising about the 'ideal team coach', with very few books on the subject and virtually nothing in the way of public discourse. At present perceptions of the role are somewhat shadowy, as was the role of the executive coach perhaps fifteen years ago.

When as a coach you are called in as the 'magic helper' to rescue a team in difficulty there is more likely to be a perceived need and a readiness to accept that help is needed than with the team that seems to be doing well. How do you:

- Negotiate your role and responsibilities with a team that may not immediately perceive your value – indeed who may see you as an unnecessary interference?
- Convince the team and yourself that you are adding value when you are apparently only intervening lightly?
- Influence an already successful team to aspire to the next level and guard against complacency?
- Persuade them that they need to work on their performance when the evidence is that they are already doing well?
- Get them to achieve the extra five per cent that could move them from good to great?

It may seem obvious to you as a coach that high performance is a fragile flower but the team may take it for granted. Highly successful sports teams and groups in the performing arts train hard to exceed their own performance expectations – there is no reason why this should not be true for the business or organisational team.

Another challenging aspect of working as a coach with successful teams is that, socially and interpersonally, they are not always comfortable places. Such teams often include pushy, driven 'alpha' types who take little care over social niceties and are impatient with anything they see as a time-wasting distraction from the job. These personalities often favour action over reflection, and frequently believe that what they have relied on to succeed in the past will necessarily get them the same results in the future, meaning they are reluctant to spend time learning, reflecting or planning. Because of their success they believe they know it all already.

In my work with individuals as an executive coach, I find this a prevalent syndrome. Even very successful leaders and professionals can reach a point where they over-rely on behaviours or qualities they see as having been instrumental in their original success. For example, those who feel they have got where they are primarily by dint of hard work can fail to recognise when a law of diminishing returns begins to apply. All my colleagues have worked with numerous burnt out executives who have failed to spot the danger signals in this area. There is also often a failure to appreciate that the strategies they have used to get as far as they have may not be the ones to use when the game changes – for example when they make the leap from implementer of operational matters to taking on a more strategic leadership role.

Team leadership and the 'vision thing'

'Whatever you can do, or dream you can, begin it! Boldness has genius, power and magic in it.'
— often attributed to Goethe, but of unknown origin

All teams, all organisations, all individuals need a sense of purpose – a reason 'why' – that will carry them through difficulty and inspire them to achieve. Responsibility for this rests primarily with the leader. Vision statements drawn from democratic processes rarely capture the imagination. I have personally facilitated numerous sessions in the past where boards or chief executive teams have set themselves to create 'vision statements' or 'mission statements'. There are few less rewarding activities than spending a day or two in a room with ten clever and strong-willed executives trying to craft a single sentence. The process is usually tortuous and the results are often anodyne and clichéd.

Some leaders can bring real inspiration to the process, usually as a result of long reflection and struggle to establish the meaning and purpose of their personal journeys. Some are never visited by inspirational vision.

But by whatever process it is achieved, vision is important. To lack vision is to risk settling for an uninspired team – and often, by extension, a poorly focused and unmotivated organisation. This is a sadly common state of affairs:

many employees have no real sense what their organisation is really *for* other than what it 'does' in the sense of the goods it produces or the service it provides. Every management guru, trainer, consultant or coach knows that if you connect someone to a sense of deeper purpose they will strive to achieve it, and that a compelling vision is a key means of creating that purpose. Consequently, leadership vision is not only a driver of organisational performance but a moral necessity. As Richard Branson writes, 'Business has to give people enriching, rewarding lives or it is simply not worth doing' (Branson, 2010).

This enrichment of the working experience begins with the leader and his or her vision – a dream and a direction that other people want to share and follow. This is not just expressed as a vision 'statement' – many of which are to be found forgotten at the bottom of office drawers – but is manifested in the actions and words of the leader. Not any old vision will do. A good vision should:

- Reflect the culture of the organisation
- Set clear direction and purpose
- Inspire loyalty
- Inspire enthusiasm, belief and commitment
- Link team members to a sense of purpose that is bigger than just themselves
- Challenge people to grow and develop

In the end vision is not about quantity but about quality and the deeper human intangibles that give purpose to life.

From vision to action

It is vitally important to connect the vision to action. I knew of a team led by a highly visionary, creative leader who could not connect his vision to a clear message about what he expected his leadership team to actually *do*. This created enormous frustration and demoralisation. On one occasion he took his team to the Lake District for a development exercise, and one late afternoon the trainer suggested a hill walk which the team would manage entirely for themselves. The result was a chaotic microcosm of how the team operated under his leadership. He walked around following his own interests and the team followed him asking him where he thought they should go. His answers were characteristically vague, and the team fragmented. Some followed the leader, others decided to go their own way, some walked back to base in frustration. The subsequent review was conducted in an atmosphere of anger and frustration with the leader getting the message that he really needed to spell out what he expected from the team individually and collectively. Merely offering creative ideas and visionary concepts was not enough.

Earning acceptance

For the coach, gaining entry, establishing credibility and getting commitment from the team to engage in development work is often the first hurdle. Often it will be the team leader who engages the coach and it is vital for the coach to be seen as impartial and working in the interests of the whole team rather than just the boss. This is a critical success factor: without being accepted by the whole team it is virtually impossible to operate effectively in the role of team coach.

A good start is to meet and interview each member of the team separately (see the section on 'learning about the team' in Chapter 2). This is an opportunity to gain rapport, build individual relationships and establish that you are there to work on behalf of the whole team, not just the leader. You can also use the opportunity to ask what would be of specific benefit to each individual – what they would each hope to get out of the process. Additionally you can take the opportunity to ask about any anxieties they might have about a team development process and to offer reassurance about the potential benefits.

A simple but highly effective technique when working with the whole team is to ask them to brainstorm potential benefits versus potential drawbacks of engaging in a team development process. This simple exercise invariably elicits far more pluses than minuses, even with a team that may harbour some scepticism. On the benefit side they will typically foresee opportunities to:

- Learn more about each other, both as people and as professionals – for example, strengths and weaknesses and the current work pressures that individuals may be experiencing
- Review performance and learn from it
- Build a climate of support
- Plan and perhaps adapt behaviour in the light of forthcoming challenges
- Build rapport and a united front in the face of organisational political pressures
- Become more influential in the organisation

On the drawback side they may express anxiety about:

- The time taken out of busy schedules
- Too much naval-gazing
- Opening a Pandora's Box of interpersonal issues.

Frequently it is the leader who has most anxiety – even if they do not show it. They may fear losing a degree of control or authority to the team coach or of being personally exposed in some way. The team coach has to win over the team leader first, and initial discussions on how a development programme might work need to be thoroughly explored, with the leader's concerns addressed, before work with the wider team can begin.

As with all team development, it is vital to gain commitment to a contract of agreed behaviours with the team members themselves.

The make-up of the team

It is comparatively rare for a team leader to inherit or select a team they see as absolutely ideal. Often they feel 'lumbered' with team members whom they would ideally prefer not to have, or with combinations of members that do not easily gel. The team may include:

- 'Leftovers' inherited from an old team who may be resistant to changing the way they work to meet the new leader's expectations
- Unwanted 'transfers' from other teams whose moves have been dictated by factors such as organisational politics
- Previous rivals for the position of team leader who were unsuccessful in their application and may therefore resent the leader
- Factions, such as groups of 'old' team members who resent the leader's new appointments

But even if the team is not one the leader would necessarily have picked from scratch, it can still be highly successful. Paying attention to team roles can have a big bearing on the degree of success the team is likely to experience. If the leader *does* have a degree of discretion over who they recruit for their team, then the theory of informal team roles described by Meredith Belbin can be of great value (Belbin, 1981). Even if the team leader has little discretion in this area, he or she can still leverage the effectiveness of the team they have by paying attention to Belbin's ideas.

Team roles

In *Management Teams: Why They Succeed or Fail*, Belbin reports on research he has conducted within organisations over several years (Belbin, 1981). The following material depends heavily on Belbin's work. Before Belbin's theories attracted general attention, recruitment of team members was often done under the assumption that teams were best made up of 'rounded' individuals, people who were seen to be able to fit comfortably into a wide range of team roles. Belbin's research indicated that rather than recruit teams made up of rounded individuals it was more effective to create rounded teams consisting of complementary individuals who, as well as offering specific skills or expertise, occupied a spread of specific but informal team roles. He also exploded the so-called 'alpha' hypothesis in which the assumption ran that putting all the cleverest people in a team would necessarily make for success: in simulations he ran, teams composed of 'alpha' types normally performed extremely poorly.

Belbin describes eight distinct team roles and an additional 'Specialist' role. With the exception of the Specialist, these are roles to do with the *processes* of team operation, rather than with the technical aspects of the work. They concern the way the team handles the process of such things as management, problem-solving and coordination. These roles are quite distinct from whatever technical contribution (such as engineering, accounting, production and so on) particular individuals may make to team functioning.

In the descriptions that follow, the role is the particular contribution that the person's strengths and preferences allow them to fill. The section on typical behaviour may help you to identify the roles which your colleagues most often play.

Chair (Coordinator): The Coordinator provides leadership (in the conventional sense of the term) by coordinating the efforts and contributions of team members. This is often a subtle form of leadership which consists of encouraging contributions from others.

Role: Controlling the way in which the team moves forward towards group objectives. Ensuring that each team member's potential is used.

Characteristics: Typically calm, self-confident and controlled.

Typical behaviour: Clarifying the goals and objectives of the group. Selecting problems on which decisions are to be made, and deciding the priorities. Helping to establish roles, responsibilities and work boundaries within the team. Summing up.

Completer-finisher: Provides attention to detail and follow-up, and instils a sense of urgency. Most usefully given the role of checking final completion of team tasks.

Role: Protecting the team from mistakes and omissions. Searching for aspects of the work which require particular attention.

Characteristics: Typically painstaking, orderly, conscientious and anxious.

Typical behaviours: Emphasising the need for task completion and the observance of targets and schedules. Looking for errors, omissions and oversights.

Implementer: The backbone of the team in accomplishing detailed and practical outcomes.

Role: Turning concepts and plans into practical working procedures. Carrying out agreed plans systematically and efficiently.

Characteristics: Typically conservative, dutiful and predictable.

Typical behaviours: Transforming talk and ideas into practical steps. Trimming ideas so that they fit agreed plans and established systems.

Monitor-Evaluator: The 'devil's advocate', criticising the ideas and suggestions offered by team members. The Monitor-Evaluator can usefully evaluate all new plans.

Role: Analysing problems. Evaluating ideas and suggestions so that the team is better placed to take balanced decisions.

Characteristics: Typically sober, unemotional and prudent.

Typical behaviours: Analysing problems and situations. Interpreting complex written material and clarifying obscurities. Assessing the judgements and contributions of others.

Plant innovator: The 'ideas person' of the team, the prime source of ideas and innovation. Is best given an innovative role where ideas can be generated.

Role: Advancing new ideas and strategies, with special attention to major issues. Looking for ways around problems that confront the team.

Characteristics: Typically creative, individualistic, serious-minded and unorthodox.

Typical behaviours: Advancing proposals of own devising. Being a source of ideas. Making criticisms that lead to counter-suggestions. Offering new insights on the lines of action already agreed.

Resource investigator: The person who develops contacts and liaises with the outside world, acting as a source of external information and ideas.

Role: Typically explores and reports on ideas and other resources from outside the team, and maintains useful external contacts.

Characteristics: Often extroverted, enthusiastic, curious and communicative.

Typical behaviours: Introducing ideas and developments from outside the team, keeping and instigating external contacts. Handling negotiations with external entities.

Shaper: Provides leadership (in the conventional sense of the term) by directing and controlling the team's members.

Role: Exerting a strong influence on the way in which the team operates and the objectives it pursues. Directing attention to such matters as setting goals and priorities.

Characteristics: Typically highly strung, outgoing, dynamic.

Typical behaviours: Shaping the team roles, boundaries, responsibilities, tasks and objectives. Pushing the group towards agreement on policy, action and decision-making.

Team worker: Maintains group harmony, member satisfaction and team spirit to maintain team effectiveness. Usefully fills support positions within a team.

Role: Supporting members in their strengths – for example, by building on their suggestions. Improving communication and fostering team spirit.

Characteristics: Typically socially orientated, rather mild, and sensitive.

Typical behaviours: Giving personal support and help to others. Building on or seconding another member's ideas and suggestions. Taking steps to avert disruption to team harmony.

One of Belbin's most important findings was that overall team effectiveness depends on the knowledge team members have of each other, and use. In particular, members of more effective teams have a better knowledge of each other's strengths and the different team roles each of them can play, and use this knowledge within the team.

Team effectiveness also depends on a balance of team roles. In the more effective teams each of a number of distinct roles is filled by at least one member. Some roles are filled better by only one person – more than one co-ordinator or shaper may interfere with team capability.

One person may fill more than one role. Some people have a number of preferred roles that are about equal in preference. They can successfully fill any of these roles. Others have a clear preferred role but with one or two 'back-up' roles which they can fill comfortably.

An effective team typically has either one coordinator or one shaper, and one each of the other team roles. With one person filling more than one role, a team of fewer than seven people is often very effective.

It is clearly advantageous for people to fill the roles for which their strengths and preferences suit them. However, for a short time many people can fill roles which are well outside their usual preferences provided they understand the importance of the role to the team's effectiveness. It also helps if they are given some say in the role they are to fill.

In those teams where there is a particular gap in the list of roles it will often be useful for the whole team to take responsibility for filling that gap. In that way, the onerous burden of doing something which does not come easily does not fall on only one person.

In some teams, all roles are fulfilled. Team functioning can still be enhanced by team members understanding their particular contribution, and learning more constructive ways of exercising it. Understanding the other roles can also make relationships more satisfying and thus lift morale.

As a team coach and leader it is not necessary to swallow Belbin's ideas whole. It is not a complete theory of teams. So much depends on the personality and behaviour of the role 'holder', not to mention the style and purpose of the team itself. As with all theory it is best used as an informer of thinking and action, not a prescription. What I have found most valuable is the practice of introducing the concept to a team with a view to facilitating a learning discussion. Most teams seem to see some validity in the concept, and occasionally it can produce real insight, explaining why specific individuals feel stressed or why the team seems to have blind spots or repeats particular kinds of mistakes.

Creating success targets

It is important for a team to have a few robust, quick and easy ways of assessing where it is currently in terms of potential for performance and of reviewing their progress.

A useful model for assessing the health of a team in terms of the effectiveness of their interpersonal communications is the Communication Pyramid (see Figure 4.1), which describes the levels at which interpersonal communications occur and where they can become blocked in groups or teams. If the leader demonstrates openness and encourages risk-taking in communications then the team has the opportunity to communicate through all the levels.

Peak performance is dependent on effective communications across all the levels, according to circumstance. Sometimes the team needs to confront difficult issues or respond effectively to challenging situations, and an open communication style is key to this. Many teams can become functionally blocked by the inability to express emotions. When this happens it can feel as if a huge amount of their energy is stifled or directed towards keeping a lid on dangerous feelings – in these teams there is often a sense that emotions could explode.

Where the leader is open and communicative the team will generally follow. The key is for the leader to establish a climate of trust – one conducive to risk-taking. This means encouraging others to put forward both their thoughts

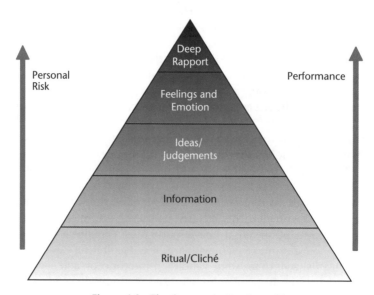

Figure 4.1 The Communication Pyramid

and feelings without fear of judgement; even mistakes should be seen as opportunities for learning.

Think about teams you are in or have been in. If you believe the boss will in some way punish you for making a mistake – even for saying something 'wrong' – the usual effect will be that you start behaving defensively and put energy into covering up your mistakes. Where the boss encourages all contributions and models free and open dialogue, then team members usually follow suit.

As a team coach you can explain the model to the team and ask them to assess their own communication 'levels' in the context of the model. Sometimes teams will say that parts of the team will communicate at more levels than other parts. This can be a cue to a discussion on how the entire team could improve its functioning through more open communication. The model can be re-visited as required for the team to conduct an informal 'health check' on its communication ability.

The model is also useful for discussing how the team might need to behave and communicate in order to welcome and integrate new team members effectively, or how to engage effectively with other teams and stakeholders.

Running effective team meetings

A lot of team business is conducted in formal meetings. I am no longer astonished at how poorly many such meetings are conducted, even when the leader is otherwise top notch and the team is talented. Agendas are often poorly constructed, people arrive late and leave early, blackberries and other mobile devices are used, and discussion moves aimlessly from topic to topic or spirals in ever-decreasing circles to miniscule levels of detail. The team meeting is often a significant point of entry for the team coach, as leaders sometimes begin an engagement with a coach by inviting them to observe the weekly meeting. For the team coach this is a powerful opportunity to see the team working at first hand, and it is often an illuminating – and sometimes shocking – experience. Some behaviours are almost unbelievable: take for example a meeting some years ago in which tension was high, yet in which most participants spent considerable time texting or emailing on mobile devices. If this was not bad enough it later transpired some team members were texting or emailing each other – and that sometimes they were exchanging insults!

It is useful to have an outline check list to assess the effectiveness of the meeting. For example:

- Does everyone arrive on time? How is lateness treated?
- Is the overall purpose of the meeting clear?
- Is there an agenda? Has it been circulated beforehand?

- Have relevant papers been circulated in advance of the meeting so that members can read them?
- Does the agenda have clarity and coherence and focus or is it essentially just a list without priorities?
- Does the agenda have expected outcomes indicated for each item or just subject headings?
- How effectively is the meeting chaired? Is there opportunity for everyone to contribute or do a minority of participants dominate?
- How is conflict dealt with? Is it suppressed, or inflamed by interpersonal issues and animosities?
- Are there clear action points arising from the meeting, with dates and names attached?

The most frequent improvements I am able to suggest are the following:

- Don't meet at all if it is just about information exchange – use other media to save time.
- Be clear about the core purpose of each meeting and include this in the agenda. Meetings can be about decisions, communications, ideas or creativity, and socialising – make sure the meeting agenda is designed to achieve its purpose.
- Make punctuality compulsory.
- Start the meeting on time and end it on time.
- Have clear outcomes stated for each agenda item, and have these outcomes posted on a flip chart so that the chair of the meeting can keep contributions relevant. This will also provide a basis for assessing how effective the meeting has been.
- Send out an agenda in advance with a clear indication of who is expected to contribute what on each agenda item so that individuals have the opportunity to prepare in advance.
- Review how each meeting has gone, and include any agreed proposals for improvements to the process in the action points from the meeting.
- Ensure that meetings are used for praise and positive feedback – leaders should follow the maxim of praising in public and criticising in private. This does not mean ignoring performance issues, however.

Sustaining high performance

It is a cliché in sport that the real challenge is not to win a championship but to stay on top, year after year. The same is true of organisational teams. Building them to a good level of performance is one thing; sustaining it is far harder. The key to sustaining high performance in a business team is to make sure the team's effort is focused on current organisational goals. This means the leader has to guard against a 'business as usual' mentality. Teams that have achieved success can slip quickly into the assumption that 'what got us here will keep us here'. With a team at the top of an organisation this will mean the leader periodically focusing its attention outwards to ensure that the organisation itself is meeting what is required of it and anticipating future challenges. In a commercial organisation this will mean scanning for market trends across a wide spectrum of products and services, looking at the big picture with an awareness that subtle consumer and social trends can affect your own organisation. One example of this is customer service. It could be that your organisation habitually benchmarks its customer service only against its direct competitors. This is a mistake, as customers who buy a wide range of goods and services will have their personal expectations set by the standards of service they receive from the whole range of suppliers and service providers they encounter, not just by the standards set by your direct competitors. It pays to benchmark your organisation's customer service standards against the best, regardless of sector.

It is also important to focus the team to think broadly about wider social trends in order to ensure they keep their thinking sharp about what the future will demand of their organisation.

Scenario planning

This began as a military planning technique and was adopted by industry in the 1970s. Scenario planning exercises can be done in highly sophisticated ways but the essence is:

- Scan your environment: what is going on politically, demographically, socially, economically, environmentally and so on?
- What are the trends that will impact your organisation?
- What are the 'critical discontinuities' – the unexpected things that *could* happen, which if they *did* happen would have huge impact for you?
- How well are you prepared to tackle both the expected trends and the critical discontinuities?

How many organisations saw the recent credit crunch and recession coming and prepared for it? We often assume that the future is going to be a default extension of how things are currently going, but history periodically throws up surprise events that radically challenge how organisations go about planning and preparing. For the leader or coach working with a successful team it is important to ensure that even when they are working like demons to keep the current momentum going they periodically take time to look at the bigger picture.

Creativity and imagination

Human beings are creatures of strong mental habit. Teams also find habitual ways of framing, discussing and dealing with the issues they face and settle on a default view of what they expect of themselves. Successes or failures are accepted as the norm and the team's view of its own power and potency reaches a limit. This is fine as long as the team is progressing but not when it is in danger of reaching a performance plateau: standing still in performance terms usually means falling behind. Intervening often requires a leader or team coach to deliberately detach part of their thinking from the team norm in order to re-envision more powerful models of performance. This is not an easy or straightforward process. Challenging current thinking, behaviour, performance and achievement levels can unsettle the team itself, key stakeholders to the team and even its customers.

Creativity can be the competitive edge that sets a team apart. Many teams shy away from the word creativity on the grounds that it can feel like a flaky concept. The reality is that creativity in organisational life is usually about finding ways to adapt – or steal – good ideas from other sources and adopt them for practical use. It is about finding tiny improvements, ways round problems and other little nuances that will sharpen its competitive edge. The truly high performing team has a culture of continuous improvement and this cannot flourish if space and time is not given to fresh thinking. This is something both the team coach and the coaching team leader can bring to the otherwise effective team – creating the opportunities to ensure that complacency and stale thinking never set in.

An example of excellence: England rugby

Clive Woodward is an instructive example of a leader/coach who did exactly this. He was appointed coach of the England rugby union team in the late 1990s. At the time of his appointment the England team was enjoying a reasonably successful spell following the work of two previous strong coaches. They were ranked around fourth or fifth in the world and would occasionally put in a bravura performance to beat one of the top teams from the southern hemisphere who were globally recognised as the giants of rugby. For Woodward this was not good enough. He was unusual in the sports coaching world in that he brought models of performance thinking from the world of business and management theory into sport: previously the traffic had tended to flow in the other direction, with businesses incorporating performance models from sports psychology.

Woodward set out to create an England team that would be number one in the world and that could win the rugby world cup. He challenged each of his players to become, individually, the best player in his position in the world. He took risks – for example, throwing in a team of largely untried youngsters against the high-ranking Australian team: he was widely criticised for this, and England were slaughtered, but he found one or two new players, including the eighteen-year-old Jonny Wilkinson, who were to become the spine of his new team. He challenged the governing hierarchy of English rugby, and insisted on the England team being given the best facilities in the world, in line with his ambition. He instilled a regime of high standards for the team in every area of their training, preparation and general conduct; those who did not like it were dispensed with. He gave huge responsibility to the players to set their own standards and improve on them, treating them like intelligent adults. The players adopted a system of mutual accountability and no-holds-barred feedback combined with fierce loyalty. Despite numerous setbacks on the playing field, and continued criticism from fans, sports journalists and former players, the hard core of a brilliant and consistent team began to form. He embraced innovation at a pace that shocked some people, including, controversially, the adoption of a new kind of 'slippery' shirt for the players that made them harder to tackle. Sometimes his innovations failed and drew sceptical responses from his senior players but that did not stop him endlessly looking for small changes that could add even one per cent to performance.

Eventually England won the World Cup in 2003 having been the number one team for two or three years prior to that. Famously, Jonny Wilkinson produced the kick that won the game in the last moments of the match – but what many people do not know is that this kick only happened because the rest of the team had won field position using tactics and mental preparation that had been years in the making. Previous England teams would probably have blown it. Following the World Cup Woodward sought even better facilities and more expensive backing for the team in his determination to improve performance levels still further. When the powers that be refused to accede to his requests he resigned. Despite having more players to draw upon than any other country, England struggled for years following his departure.

Summary

The very best teams can leave you breathless with admiration. They can appear like invincible champions. But the truth is their effectiveness is never a matter of luck or of simply assembling gifted people – in fact Belbin's early findings showed that the team built on the assumption that sheer talent would prevail were often the weakest kind of team. Excellence is built on the right processes, structures and habits – including the habit of creative renewal and critical appraisal.

Learning points

- The high-performing team can be the toughest to lead or coach.
- High performance can never be taken for granted but must be continuously worked on – it is a fragile flower.
- High performance in a team depends on everyone accepting responsibility.
- Supposedly 'soft' concepts like vision and creativity are at the heart of high performance – high performers rarely do 'business as usual'.

Reflective questions

- Consider the best teams you have been in – what really made them great?
- What might you need to bring to your game to lead and coach a high performing team?
- What might a discerning critic say about your coaching or leadership approach?
- What can you learn from effective leaders and coaches you have known?

5 Handling the problematic team

'Success is the ability to go from one failure to another with no loss of enthusiasm.'

– Winston Churchill

All teams can be said to be problematic in some way – in the sense that there is never a perfect team – but in this chapter we look at teams that are seriously dysfunctional. These might represent less than ten per cent of the teams I have worked with but their impact on me has been powerful, as has been the opportunity to learn from them. It is possible to learn more from failures than from successes – both of course subjective terms and 'twin imposters'. Things are rarely clear cut and some of the teams I have judged as problematic have been viewed from the outside as star performers.

One of the most challenging aspects of working with a seriously dysfunctional team as a coach is the need to manage and look after oneself. It is only too possible to get drawn into the drama, become seduced by the idea of being the saviour of the hopeless team, or suffer anxiety and guilt at their failure to make progress. There may be days when you feel you simply cannot face them – when fear of their hostility or frustration with their intransigence causes personal stress. In retrospect there are one or two teams I stayed with through thick and thin that I should have simply walked away from. Likewise there are individuals within teams you encounter who can drive you to despair despite every intellectual conviction you may hold about the value, resourcefulness or potential in every human being. I include some tips on managing oneself in the very challenging situations that working with teams can present.

Goal-setting with problematic teams

A lot is made of the goal-setting process in all aspects of coaching. You can take it as read that I conscientiously negotiated goals for my work with all the teams I describe here. But sometimes it is only when you get into the work and start to uncover some of the deeper and more troubling issues that you realise how superficial a process goal-setting can be. At the initial diagnostic stage it can be the case that 'naming' of dysfunctional behaviours is too difficult for the team – even for the leader, who in any case may be part of the problem. It is important to have a framework of goals at the beginning of an intervention, but also to keep open the possibility of renegotiating these when and if the true nature of the team's issues becomes evident.

Macho teams

Outright machismo in teams is by no means a thing of the past and by no means confined to male behaviour. A macho team can be tough, dynamic, exciting and powerful but at the same time fear-ridden, brutal and narrow-minded. The term 'macho' may be judged by some readers as pejorative but here it is not intended to be. All teams have their strengths and weaknesses, and in some contexts macho teams can be stunningly successful, full of fun and indeed a force for good. At other times they can be myopic, chauvinistic and even dangerous. Signs of the problematic version of the macho team include:

- A preponderance of extrovert behaviour coupled with intolerance for introversion
- 'Mickey-taking', often savage in nature, as the predominant form of humour
- A tendency to use 'win-lose' language and 'business is war' metaphors
- Casual sexism and sometimes other 'isms' too
- An intolerance for intellectual or reflective activity
- Impatience with lengthy planning or analysis
- A high preponderance of driven, even ruthless individuals
- Ruthless and sometimes reactive or impulsive decision-making
- Behind the superficial togetherness an underlying philosophy of 'look after number one'

Case study one: The Robber Barons

This was a team of high-flying media executives. When I first went to see them to discuss a team-coaching assignment I was asked to address the whole team at the end of one of their weekly meetings. Apart from the Chief Executive I had met none of them in advance, but knew the reputations of several of them – which were daunting to say the least. I was ushered into a room full of smoke and laughter, was vaguely introduced, and proceeded to lay out my stall in an atmosphere akin to that of a sixth-form common room or the Drones club of PG Wodehouse. Jokes were bandied about, almost everything I said attracted a wise-crack, various sub-groups of the team chattered to each other throughout, and from time to time paper missiles were hurled through the air from one team member to (or rather *at)* another. Questions to me were delivered with a withering cynicism: some questions were so tortuously 'clever' and multiple they became unanswerable. Several of the team made no secret of the fact they considered their time was being wasted even before they had heard what I had to say.

Key scene

On a team development programme with this team, I set up an exercise called Red/Blue (see Chapter 6: Designing interventions). The point of the exercise was to look at issues of trust and interdependency within the team – something I felt to be really important given that they were prone to backstabbing. I divided the team by an arbitrary process into two smaller groups. Each group occupied a separate room, but was given an identical instruction sheet. The exercise offered the opportunity for each group to signal to the other either co-operation (win-win) or competition (win-lose, or even lose-lose). If they both independently signalled cooperation they would both win. If either or both groups signalled competition, one or both would lose according to the scoring of the game. I spent a little time with each group to ensure they understand the rules and to observe their initial discussions. In one of the groups an excited woman pronounced her view on how her group should approach the game. 'Right!' she exclaimed, 'it's simple! F*** or be f*****!'

Both groups proceeded to play every possible trick on each other. They even went back on their word – accompanied by handshakes and solemn promises – to cooperate following a mid-game conference. Needless to say, both groups lost as they brought each other down.

The review of this exercise was unique in my career. Normally a review would take a maximum of thirty minutes. This one took over half a day. It provided an opportunity to raise all sorts of grievances between individuals and was one of the most emotionally charged sessions I had ever experienced with a team. Ultimately the catharsis was beneficial but it took every ounce of resourcefulness on my part to keep the session on something like an even keel. The key was to agree and enforce a contract of behaviour and protocol which stipulated that each group should have its say without interruption from the other group, and for me to write this agreement on a flip chart and enforce it rigorously.

The team actually made progress from this experience – for example, in agreeing that it was no longer acceptable to secretly lobby the leader for personal interests outside of the regular team meetings. Characteristically the team could not accept this new agreement without at the same time 'sending it up' with their wickedly irreverent humour. Immediately after agreement on this policy had been struck we had a break. As the team leader left the room one wag said, 'Where's he gone – and who's gone with him?'

Organisational, cultural and systemic factors

This team existed in the context of a large public broadcasting body. Within this organisation they controlled perhaps the jewels in the crown. Their department enjoyed the highest status both within the organisation and in the eyes and ears of the UK viewing and listening public. Some of the top team were public figures who would appear regularly in the press – not least in *Private Eye*, the satirical magazine. Relationships that some of the managers held outside the organisation, such as with politicians and media figures, clearly had a bearing on internal politics – if a certain member of the team was said to be 'in' with some important political figure it had significant bearing on their internal influence too. It was as if the organisation had no walls. The senior management of the wider organisation operated in a highly political and elitist way, with the most senior managers behaving at times as if they were part of a Hollywood depiction of the Roman senate: staff within the organisation were constantly speculating as to who was 'in' or 'out', or who was thought to be plotting what with whom. A common metaphor used by staff for the senior management cadre was that of the medieval court. The team I was working with was frequently referred to as 'the robber barons' due to the widespread perception that they were ruthlessly politicised empire builders.

What I tried to do

I worked with this team in the end for a couple of years or more. In this time I acted in all the roles a team coach is called upon to fill at various times. As a *process consultant* I undertook diagnostic exercises. Some of these were to form the basis of strategic and operational discussions and resulted in policy changes. As a *team builder* I organised events involving exercises and simulations designed to build mutual trust and understanding and skills of communication and cooperation. As an *executive coach* I worked with the chief executive and several of the individual members of the team on issues such as problem-solving, how to lead *their* teams, confidence in making important presentations and numerous other issues. I also used a coaching style in asking the team to address various questions about the way they worked together. As a *facilitator* I helped design and run several events aimed at helping them understand and organise their work more strategically and effectively, and to address specific organisational problems and issues.

Specific challenges

The key issues for me in my role of team coach were:

- Establishing and maintaining personal credibility and acceptance
- Dealing with direct aggression and cynicism
- Coping with their very short attention span and limited patience for anything even remotely reflective
- Ensuring I was not seen as the personal 'creature' or stooge of the chief executive
- Ensuring I did not collude with their behaviour

My response to these challenges

I would have to confess to experiencing a good deal of apprehension – even fear – when working with this team. They could de-rail a serious discussion with a wickedly funny remark, explode into anger at the drop of a hat or simply refuse to play ball if they did not agree with my ideas and suggestions. On the other hand they could be exhilarating and inspiring, and they partied like there was no tomorrow at a time in my career when I still thought that staying up all night was fun. It was like trying to stay mounted on a bucking bronco.

I do not pretend to have been successful in all aspects of my work with this team – there were one or two near-disasters and a couple of individuals I never seemed to establish rapport with, one of them a notorious bully. In as much as the coaching was successful it boiled down to persistence. There were a couple of times when I felt I could not face them again. In the end I think they respected the fact that I kept turning up and kept reminding them of the same things – how they had promised to work together, what their success depended on and the behaviours that could sabotage their success. One of them remarked that I was like a priest to the team, holding them to their responsibilities and commitments and acting as their conscience. In addition it was important to be able to take a joke against myself – too thin a skin and I would not have made it past the first meeting. Sometimes I and the other coaches who worked with this team had to find the courage to say the unsayable – naming the elephant in the room. There were numerous occasions when it fell to us to point out terrible behaviour – perhaps on the part of one of the bullies in the team. It was really helpful to enlist the help of a colleague from time to time to assist in individual events and exercises. Sometimes I just needed moral support, at others a fresh view on the team and how I was working with them. This is a practice I would strongly recommend for someone working with a particularly challenging team over a long period – it can be lonely as a team coach and it is also possible to lose perspective.

None of the above behaviours is associated with any particular body of psychological or organisational theory. However, throughout the assignment it was important to be able to draw on these theories in order to keep perspective and to provide a certain amount of reassurance that we were on track.

Results of the work

In the end we made tangible progress. Sometimes it is hard to measure progress in any meaningful way but in this case there were some definite wins, including:

- A more ordered and widely understood approach to managing their collective work
- Better run team meetings with better behaviour
- At least the basis for better listening and dialogue – although they would revert to macho type at times of pressure
- A better sense of collective discipline and interdependence
- Increased understanding of, and support for, the work of individuals

Case study two: The Emperors of Europe

This team was likewise a group of senior broadcasting executives, but from a very different part of the industry – and from a completely separate organisation. If this team did not have the outright machismo of the robber barons there were several in the team who more than made up for it by the intensity of their interpersonal competitiveness. Much of this was conducted under the guise of playful jocularity; and indeed they were mostly a funny and charming group of people, witty in the extreme. For three of the team in particular, however, the fun did not seem to stop at playful verbal jousting. In the sessions we ran it became clear that much of the energy of the group was directed at these running battles. We learned that, outside of the sessions, the three were engaged in constant politicising to gain kudos, pre-eminence and influence with their boss and with other 'players' in the wider organisation.

Key scene

The team was reviewing a problem-solving exercise intended to focus attention on listening, involvement and, above all, the need to encourage contribution from *everyone* in the group. The exercise and review had been set up specifically to allow the team the opportunity to discuss the fact that some members frequently struggled to get a chance to speak – and that consequently their contributions were sometimes completely lost during team meetings and discussions. The team did not succeed in the task. Once the exercise was over, I asked them to review how they had approached the problem as a team. As the exercise review developed, attention became focused almost entirely on the technical aspects of the exercise – on how they should have solved the problem. The dominant members of the group began arguing about how they had conducted the exercise in terms of decisions they had made and how they had intellectually failed to solve the puzzle the exercise had set them, each trying to blame the other for failure. I tried to draw their attention to some of the process factors – critically, the fact that because a few of the group had dominated 'airspace' throughout the exercise some of the team had hardly got a word in and had been unable to share important information, without which the exercise could not be solved. The behaviour in the review became a direct reflection of the behaviour in the exercise which had itself been a reflection of how the team worked in meetings. Eventually the point got home: in fact the team leader later said it had been a breakthrough moment and one they used as a reference point in future meetings.

Organisational, cultural and systemic factors

This team were part of a global media organisation – and the metaphor of 'empire' seemed to underpin much of the internal politics of the organisation. They were collectively in charge of the European region of the organisation and there was little doubt that they saw it essentially as an empire to be ruled. Many of the individuals looked to sources of power and influence outside of the team as a means to further their own careers, courting the attention of seniors within the organisation or other powerful media figures. As a result, some of them did not see much to be gained from committing their full attention and energy to the team, despite the fact that our sessions clearly established a practical need for interdependent behaviours and attitudes.

What I tried to do

Despite the self-centredness of some team members this was essentially a happy and spirited team. They were much easier to work with than the robber barons and were much more willing to learn and adapt their behaviours – possibly because on average they were about ten years younger. The main coaching input was to:

- Offer feedback about their behaviour
- Create structured sessions in which they could explore and address some specific counter-productive behaviours
- Provide models and measures against which they could check their progress

- Create some boundaries and hold a safe space in which they could address uncomfortable issues

Results of the work

Perhaps the main outcome was that two of the more maverick players left in order to further their careers elsewhere. It may not be possible to attribute their decisions directly to the coaching intervention, but they had been brought to heel by their boss and colleagues and this contributed to their departure.

Over time the team became more organised, listened better and created space for the quieter members of the team to contribute. The quieter members of the team became much more settled and happy to contribute.

Case study three: The Three Amigos

This was a team of investment bankers. I worked with the wider team only a few times, but worked with the three most senior members of the team more frequently. Unlike the witty banter employed by the two media-based teams, their humour was blunt and dark – some of it just a fraction short of outright abuse. The key dynamic within the trio was the domineering behaviour of two of the senior members of the team towards the third, and it was this issue that was to form the centrepiece of my work with them.

Key scene

Picture the tranquil yet stirring scenery at Brathay Hall, a leadership development centre using the outdoors, situated in the English Lake District on the northern shore of Lake Windermere. Outside the main building a team of senior investment bankers on a team-building exercise is preparing to undertake a warm-up exercise on the first evening of their course. They are laughing and joking, 'taking the mickey' out of each other. I hand one of the team a sheet of paper on which are written the instructions for the exercise.

The task is for the whole team to traverse a two-inch wide ledge that runs above the ground on the side wall of the hall. The instructions make it very clear that the team succeeds only if everyone makes it to the other end of the wall without falling off – a drop of fifteen inches. The task is designed to encourage team planning, communication 'down the line', and above all, mutual support. As a warm-up exercise, it is not supposed to be too difficult – I have seen numerous teams, including teams of disadvantaged teenagers, succeed purely by dint of working together as a unit and offering hands on support in a literal sense.

The team leader snatches the paper out of the hands of the team member I have handed it to, reads it cursorily, throws it to the ground and announces, 'Right, it's easy – we just need to get along the ledge!' At which point chaos ensues as the team runs at the task, some attempting it individually, others conversing loudly in ones and twos. At the crux point, a bricked-in window sill that affords a resting place and anchor point, the leader and another member of the team almost wrestle to get the best position. 'Get off my ledge you *******!' shouts the team leader. One after another the team members drop to the ground. One agile person makes it to the end, and exultantly punches the air, oblivious to the fact the team has failed abjectly in terms of the task set. He is derided by his colleagues.

Organisational, cultural and systemic factors

I had had no direct experience of working inside the organisation before working with the team. In their industry:

- The weak 'went to the wall' – and were deemed to have deserved it.
- The central ethos was 'every man for himself'.
- The sexes referred and related to each other with habitual hostility.
- Elitism and arrogance were seen as good things; sensitivity or tact were signs of weakness.

In this cultural context it was predictable that bullying would take place and that 'teamwork' – and team-building in particular – would attract scepticism if not cynicism.

What I tried to do

At the time I was working as a team-building trainer, and the initial remit was to run a short course with the team. The course consisted of a structured sequence of mainly outdoor activities and review discussions designed to build group rapport and mutual understanding and to enhance the way they worked together operationally. The outstanding feature of the course was the serious dysfunction that showed up between the team's three most senior figures. During the course itself this relationship emerged as something that was demoralising and counter-productive for the team as a whole and although we addressed it to some extent on the course itself via feedback and review discussions the leader contacted me after the course to ask if I would do some further work with these three.

I met with them several times for short sessions as a trio and for coaching as individuals, during which it emerged that the domineering and even bullying behaviour of two of the team was seriously undermining the confidence and personal well-being of the third, a much quieter, introverted man. To their credit the other two came to recognise that their behaviour was often unpleasant, was counter-productive and ultimately unacceptable. The breakthrough moment was when I used a visualisation exercise with the quieter team member which revealed to him how he could stand up to the other two. Once he was better able to stand up for himself the whole balance within the trio, and the dynamic of the wider team, changed for the better. When the two tried their bullying tactics they were resisted and as a result did not try them again. All three ultimately agreed that the balance of power and the climate of their relationships together improved as a result of this intervention.

Results of the work

This was an early experience for me of combining individual coaching with training and the outcome was gratifying. The team moved from teetering on the edge of total dysfunction to a much healthier balance of interpersonal power and as a result became more stable and productive. I stayed in contact with the trio for some time after the initial work finished and they all recognised it as a breakthrough experience.

Case study four: The Toxic Health Specialists

I was asked to work with a team of eminent consultants from the National Health Service. The human resources manager who briefed my colleague warned us that the assignment was likely to be a tough one, as the team seemed to be at constant war with itself. In fact she had recommended that we work as a pair so that we would provide back-up for each other, which meant the organisation would have to pay double the fee – very unusual behaviour indeed in a context where almost every organisation, and particularly those in the public sector, is looking to cut rather than increase costs.

One reason for this willingness to pay for two team coaches rather than one was that the team's issues had started to damage the reputation of the wider organisation. There was disquiet at local, regional and national level. Such was the level of animosity within the team itself that there had even been letters to the press from one member of the team denouncing another. Various efforts at improving the climate and behaviour of the team had failed – although arguably these efforts had been far too little and far too late to prevent bad behaviour over a long period of time. Our intervention was seen as the 'last chance saloon' before an official management intervention that would almost certainly mean dismissal or enforced transfer for some of the team, along with a damaging public scandal. In retrospect, we felt we were expected to fail, and hiring us was primarily about the management being seen to do the 'right' thing, demonstrating that they had left no stone unturned in the effort to find a solution to the team's issues before initiating a formal disciplinary process. We were chosen as a female-male combination in response to concerns that there were sexist behaviours we might have to confront.

Despite the negative signals surrounding the assignment we decided to have a go at helping the team, but resolved to be wary of getting into a situation where we felt no progress could be made.

We undertook a diagnostic exercise, interviewing each member of the team to establish their perspective on the team's issues. The initial prospect was not encouraging: there were subjective reports of harassment, rudeness, aggression, racism, sexism and all manner of bullying behaviour. The issues were complex. For example, one of the consultants most frequently described as sexist or chauvinistic was from an ethnic minority. He complained of racist attitudes from other team members, both male and female.

The main presenting issue was the way private work was managed around health service duties. Some of the team were of the opinion that others were doing too much private work at the expense of their public responsibilities, but there were other more subtle issues concerning how private work was sought and obtained and how work was allocated, shared and managed. There were also issues around the management of the team; what management there was seemed largely ineffectual and the team was broadly left to its own devices.

Organisational cultural and systemic factors

It was important for us to see this team in the broader organisational context. It seemed that little direct management of the consultants had happened in the past: they were expected to handle the majority of the specialist area in which they worked. These consultants had historically enjoyed an exalted status, and they seemed to be regarded as almost above the need for direct management. 'Taking them on' was seen as a daunting task for management. In turn the consultants saw the management as 'suits' whose role was primarily to interfere.

What we tried to do

Following the diagnostic exercise we compiled a simple report, naming no names, summing up the concerns expressed. We first met with the whole team for a day, at a splendid luxury hotel that seemed to us to have been chosen with the intention of playing up to the perceived status of the consultants. The atmosphere was ultra-tense. Some of the group were friendly and welcoming – with an almost pleading quality in their expressions, as if they were hoping against hope for us to rescue them from their plight. Some were more hostile, their hostility expressed not as overt aggression but as a disinclination to engage with us beyond a very basic level of cold civility. One man in particular seemed to want to avoid any meaningful interaction. He had an unsettling, abrupt and vaguely menacing manner that conveyed strongly to us an attitude of exasperation bordering on contempt for us and the process.

After we had had some initial discussion, centring on our wish to help the team resolve its issues, we began the process of *contracting* (see the section on contracting in Chapter 2). We expressed a view to the team that much of what seemed to be wrong stemmed not so much from the issues that were swirling around as from the way in which they discussed them – or failed to discuss them. We fed back to them our perception that views and opinions seemed to have polarised and hardened over time, and that this hardening was exacerbated by the adversarial manner in which issues were debated. We believed that progress was unlikely unless we addressed the way in which the team communicated together. We introduced the idea of following the rules of *dialogue* rather than those of *debate* as below:

Principles of effective dialogue	Principles of adversarial debate
Active listening as a core principle	No real listening, just waiting to talk
Equality of participation – every person's perspective treated with respect	Perspectives of others regarded as targets to be attacked
No threat of retribution or coercion permitted	Overt or underlying power-play behaviours abound
No preconceived outcomes are assumed and the working assumption is that there may be numerous possible outcomes	Different parties or individuals assert there is one 'right' way or 'truth'
Open agendas – the aim is to deal openly with issues and to engage in authentic communication	Closed agendas – parties or individuals seeking to gain advantage by argument or rhetoric

It was our hope that we could influence the group to consider that the quality of their communication was hampering any attempt to make progress towards a solution that the whole team could live with. Basic skills seemed to be lacking too – those of attentive listening for example – and we offered, as respectfully as we could, to coach the team towards more skilful dialogue. The response to this invitation met a mixed response. Some welcomed it as a positive step towards breaking deadlock, others either labelled it a waste of time or offered lip-service compliance combined with negative body language. We confronted these negative responses, but could not seem to break through to get full commitment.

However, after the first day we received enough positive feedback from enough of the team to convince us to carry on. We ran two or three more sessions aimed at both facilitating a resolution to their issues and improving the way they spoke to each other and worked together, but we never made conclusive progress. Something would always drag us back to bad feeling – usually one or two of the team who would fall out, argue and blame each other. Challenging them and holding them to our behavioural contract seemed to have only a temporary effect.

Results of the work

In the end we decided we could not in all conscience carry on working with them unless they agreed to end the arguing and begin working to create a new future. The final session was dramatic. We offered a summary of how we saw things in terms of potential for the future but also in terms of feedback on their behaviour and gave a gentle ultimatum. We were open about our sense of frustration and disappointment but avoided blaming. We said we would go for a walk around the garden for an hour whilst they discussed whether or not they were prepared to commit to a fresh start under agreed rules for behaviour. If they were prepared to commit to this we would carry on working with them, but if not we said we would need to end the assignment. When we got back to them they said they wanted to carry on working with us. But within minutes the arguments resumed much as before, so reluctantly we wished them good luck and left. This was not easy for us emotionally – we felt to some extent as if we had failed and in particular felt guilt at letting down those members of the team who had looked to us for salvation. It was hard not to feel angry about the behaviour of one or two individuals who had been particularly difficult, but in retrospect it was a combination of their personalities within a tangled and unhappy web of history and unresolved cultural and organisational factors that were to blame.

Case study five: The Editorial Team and the Smiling Assassin

This assignment arose out of a one-to-one executive coaching engagement. I was coaching 'Martin', the senior manager of a media department, and as we worked together Martin became clearer that his team of senior editors was not functioning as he wished. They did not seem to want to act as a strategic leadership team and instead seemed focused primarily on their separate areas of responsibility. Even more worrying for him was that the department was being asked to make extremely radical changes to the way it operated, and he was concerned that his team was neither supportive of the changes nor entirely supportive of him as their manager, choosing at times to regard him as the mouthpiece of 'the suits' – their disparaging term for senior management. In addition they did not seem to have the leadership skills he felt they needed to drive through the changes. In short, as he saw it, they were not up to the task and not up *for* it either.

As discussion continued it became clear that one individual in the team in particular, 'Kevin', was a cause for concern. This man was a senior editor of strong professional reputation and talent, and someone whom editorially Martin would find it hard to do without – in editorial terms he was a star player. Their relationship was complex and at times troubled. One factor behind this was that both had applied for the senior management job, having previously worked as peers, and Martin was concerned that Kevin resented this. Through the course of our one-to-one coaching Martin became increasingly convinced that Kevin was undermining him whilst superficially offering support. It was against this context that I agreed to undertake a team coaching intervention.

Organisational, cultural and systemic factors

This team was part of a politicised organisation where a manager's final decision was often said to be the trigger for twenty of the best brains in the country to work out how they were going to get round it. They operated in the same organisation as the robber barons but in a completely different department. They were much lower profile and not subject to public scrutiny in anything like the same way. One consistent pressure on the team was a constant downward push on costs.

What I tried to do

I interviewed the leader and each member of the team separately to find out their views about a range of issues such as:

- How they viewed the changes they were being asked to implement
- How they experienced working as a team
- What they thought of Martin as a leader
- What they thought were the key issues they needed to address

I wrote a brief summary report, in which were highlighted some of the sensitive areas the team should address. One of these was dissatisfaction felt by some of the team, especially Kevin, with the decision of Martin to hire a new commercial manager to boost the team's business management capability. She had told me during a one-to-one interview session that she felt undermined and sidelined by the team, and particularly by Kevin. The hostility with which she felt she had been greeted had caused her to question her decision to join the team.

I then held a short series of team sessions to discuss this and other issues. The sessions felt slightly unreal. I knew from the individual interviews that there was strong dissent and discomfort – particularly in relation to the new appointment – yet the tone was one of harmonious cooperation that somehow never seemed to get anywhere. I tried a range of facilitative strategies aimed at bringing the real tensions to the surface but somehow the discussion would always slide into a less critical area. I tried 'naming' this very issue, suggesting that there was some avoidance going on, but with no effect. Eventually the new appointee burst into tears and ran out of the room. I adjourned the session while Martin the manager tried to find out what was upsetting her.

She never returned to the team session and subsequently resigned her post. The rest of the team reviewed the incident, but only in a superficial way and with an implication that her behaviour showed she had been unsuitable for the job in the first place. It was only over time that I pieced together the story, and it is one in which there are very few objective facts. Reading between the lines, her life had been made a misery, by Kevin in particular, who had shouted at her, obstructed her in business matters and tried to turn the rest of the team against her. In the public sessions he had been reasonable in all his conversations. This seemed to be a pattern in his dealings with Martin too. In public sessions he was all reasonableness and charm, but rumour had him as someone who would frequently besmirch Martin's name in private.

Results of the work

The team was able to do some important transactional work about how to manage the new demands on the department. This was practical work around clarifying roles, tasks, timetables and priorities. There was also some useful work on how the team members would support each other. What was never fully grasped was the elusive nettle of Kevin's destructive behaviour.

The great lesson of this encounter for me was that there is little to be done as a team coach in a situation where someone is determined not to play it straight but is resolutely and ruthlessly pursuing a personal agenda.

Case study six: The Meltdown Team

This was another case in which a team had apparently been left to 'go bad' by senior management over a period of time. A coach was again called in as a last resort before a new chief executive would take decisive disciplinary action if no substantial improvement in team behaviour and performance could be achieved. The chief executive's account was of a team completely at war with itself. There were stories of bullying, backstabbing and even blackmail. The reputation not only of this team but of the whole trust was at stake.

I was asked to undertake a diagnostic exercise aimed at exploring the feasibility of mounting some form of remedial team development exercise. This was the team's last chance.

I embarked on what proved to be an emotionally gruelling sequence of interviews with each individual member of the team over two days. During this time my thoughts and feelings were twisted this way and that as each individual gave their side to the story. Some just wanted to express their distress and anxiety. Others were suspicious of the whole process and were keen to keep as much of their own involvement in the team's difficulties at arm's length.

A significant few of the most powerful players were keen to lay the blame on each other, and to win me over to their version of the state of affairs. This was a disturbing and stressful couple of days. Some of the allegations made – for example, that one consultant had tried to blackmail another by telling his wife about a claimed affair – were far beyond the normal remit of a team coach.

In this particular case I felt that the level of toxicity went well beyond the realms of what could be addressed by team coaching. It was hard not to feel sorry for some of the people in the team who were suffering at the hands of a minority. But there were sinister undertones to the way in which a small handful of the team spoke to me and I felt somewhat threatened. Based on an initial gut feeling and subsequent reflective analysis, I decided to file a report to the chief executive to the effect that in my opinion the team was not in a state where it could benefit from a conventional intervention.

Toxic teams

'Toxic' is a strong word to use in the context of a team of professionals. However, from time to time (thankfully only rarely) one will come across teams where the word is truly apt. The symptoms of the toxic team are varied and numerous but include some or all of the following factors in varying degrees:

- Blaming, bullying and scapegoating
- A large element of the 'undiscussable' within the team – items deemed too difficult to raise but which permeate the atmosphere, creating tension
- Cliques and 'in-crowds'
- Favouritism from the boss
- 'Double talk' – individuals saying one thing to some colleagues and another thing to others
- Talking about – and badmouthing – colleagues behind their backs
- Lack of openness in discussions – particularly around disclosure of feelings
- Lack of clarity on values, processes and protocols, leading to lack of agreement on what is acceptable conduct
- Unfair distribution of work

- Pre-occupation with internal disputes and issues at the expense of focus on the work at hand
- Dominance of selfish or trouble-making team members

These are just some of the causes and symptoms. From a coach's perspective, toxicity is something one senses early on in an assignment. Sometimes it can be felt in the guarded or negative remarks made by a team leader in an initial contracting discussion: or when walking into a team meeting for the first time and finding the atmosphere sullen, tense or even actively hostile.

What causes toxicity in teams?

The causes of toxicity are difficult to pin down: organisations are complex systems and the dynamics of teams are complex too. All sorts of factors play a part – cultural, political, interpersonal and intrapersonal. Within my own experience I would highlight the following factors, bearing in mind that the causes are often complex:

Example one: the team left 'to rot' by senior managers
This is a syndrome that seems to happen mainly in large public organisations, including government ministries, the health service, local authorities and parts of the media. Cases vary widely, but the common denominator in my experience is that senior teams of specialists, such as hospital consultants, senior civil servants or journalists, are left largely unmanaged and fall into a dysfunctional and ultimately toxic state. The organisation effectively turns a blind eye to them until it is too late, at which point a team development specialist is sometimes called in to clear up the mess caused by managerial neglect. The trap for the team coach is to be seduced into taking on the dirty work of the senior management and risking taking the blame if the team continues to fail.

Example two: the poorly constructed team
Some teams lack clarity of role and accountability, with members who are primarily linked emotionally and politically to other parts of the organisation. This can be particularly true with project teams set up from different parts of an organisation. The trap for the team development specialist is to fail to understand the political complexities that underpin poor team behaviour and instead focus only on interpersonal dynamics and visible behaviours.

Example three: the team with an impossible task
Organisational pressure to produce and perform can have a devastating effect on the health and capability of teams and individuals within them. Sometimes whole organisations twist themselves into knots, re-organising and re-structuring in various ways as a means of avoiding the unspeakable truth

that they simply cannot achieve what is being asked of them. This is particularly true when they are high profile organisations under constant media scrutiny and subject to relentless government pressure. I would include some of our major public organisations in this category – it is simply not seen as acceptable for their senior managers to declare that government targets are unachievable. What results is the kind of double-think associated with totalitarian states – individuals talking in public as if they are doing what is needed to address issues and make progress, whilst in private knowing they cannot ultimately succeed. I have coached scores of chief executives and directors within this sector over the past fifteen years or so and many of them, whilst 'game' and committed, express real despair and anguish about the harsh and unfair climate in which they are expected to operate. I take my hat off to them.

Example four: the power of sociopaths and toxic individuals

Some people seem to thrive on creating trouble, accruing power and influence and even deliberately causing pain to others. This is an area in which there are some uncomfortable issues for a broadly liberal society in which labelling can be seen as pejorative. As professionals many of us have known, and perhaps suffered at the hands of, individuals within the teams in which we work who seem to be just plain nasty either some of the time or much of the time. Their behaviour confuses, angers or intimidates us. Sometimes these individuals are strikingly charismatic, plausible and even charming. They can be popular in parts of their peer group whilst making the lives of others they target a misery. Essentially they act entirely selfishly and *without conscience,* ruthlessly exploiting colleagues who may not even be able to understand the extent of their egocentricity.

The sad reality seems to be that there is a small but significant proportion of people in the workforce who can be justly described as sociopathic. There is a growing expert literature on this subject. Claims as to the extent of the problem vary from author to author but, shockingly, various estimates as to the number of sociopaths in the population lie between one per cent and four per cent.

The orthodoxies of psychology and our common assumptions about human motivation do not apply in conventional ways to these people and we need to learn to deal with them differently. This is not the place for detailed analysis of the subject but I would refer interested readers to the works of authors such as Robert Hare (Hare, 1993), Martha Stout (Stout, 2005) and George Simon (Simon, 1996). They provide analysis of the issues and practical guidelines for protecting yourself against these predators in the workplace.

Handling difficult behaviours

Each situation needs to be judged on its own merits. If there were such a thing as a completely fool-proof technique I would have bought it by now. What works well in one situation may not be guaranteed to work in another. Here are some 'classic' difficult team behaviours and some ideas for dealing with them effectively. Many of the behaviours and the interventions are interchangeable – you may use an intervention from the right hand column with more than one of the behaviours in the left hand column. It is important to remember to intervene in a neutral and non-judgemental way, even if you personally feel a particular behaviour is unhelpful. A useful start point is to work from the assumption that every behaviour has a positive intention, if only for the perpetrator. This is not an excuse for difficult behaviour but is useful in thinking about the possible motivation for it and is a prerequisite for challenging it in a genuinely respectful way. Of course, assumptions like this are not intellectually provable but they are certainly effective in promoting positive responses to challenging situations.

Behaviour	Ideas for intervention
The team goes quiet when a sensitive issue is discussed – it seems difficult for them to even talk about the issue.	Offer 'Feedback in the moment' along these lines: 'May I offer some feedback here? I notice that when we come to discuss this issue the level and volume of discussion goes down. The effect on me is to make me feel concerned that this issue is somehow difficult to discuss and I am wondering if that is what you are feeling.'
One or more 'loud' members of the team dominate discussion, perhaps interrupting others when they try to speak.	Name the issue as a means of challenging it: 'John, I've noticed that on several occasions when Lucy and Mike have tried to speak you have interrupted them. I am concerned they are not getting an opportunity to have their say.'
Members of the group engage in personally abusive rowing.	Remind them of the behavioural contract (see the section on contracting in Chapter 2) and of their commitment to it.
A team member's body language contradicts what he/she is actually saying.	Offer feedback in the moment *and* an element of self-disclosure such as: 'Jean, may I offer you some feedback here? I noticed that when Tony asked everyone for a positive commitment to this action you said *yes* – but at the same time your eyes looked up to the ceiling and you shook your head. I am worried that maybe you are not fully committed.'
A team member angrily confronts you as the team coach.	Begin by assuming that somewhere along the line their motivation is positive, summarise the essence of what they have said in a respectful way and ask, 'What is behind your concern here, Sheila?' This often reveals a legitimate underlying concern that you can validate without necessarily conceding ground.

Behaviour	Ideas for intervention
Someone is persistently late for team sessions.	Point out the disruptive affect in a respectful way. Refer to the team contract if relevant. Ask the team to express their views.
A team member persistently demands attention for their own issues at the expense of air time for the whole team.	Try using feedback in the moment, describing their behaviour in literal, non-judgemental terms and your concerns about the impact of the behaviour on the team and the session.

Self management

An essential precursor to dealing with these difficult behaviours is to be in control of yourself. The team coach needs to be able to handle a complex and ever-changing set of situations, often amidst strong currents of group emotion. This work needs to be carried out confidently, flexibly and respectfully and this cannot be done if the coach is feeling vulnerable, nervous or otherwise lacking in resourcefulness. The team coaching role is demanding physically, emotionally and intellectually – and sometimes ethically.

In coaching it is important to be clear where your own mental energy is going – and what you are attached to (what you need and want) emotionally. The core *principles* of both individual and team coaching are primarily intellectual in nature, but below the surface we each have our own emotional selves to manage. It is important to be clear about, and work towards, emotional attachments that are beneficial to the clients and healthy for the coach. Here is an aspirational list.

The coach should aim to be:

Attached to . . .	Detached from . . .
Listening	Interpreting
Your team succeeding	You succeeding for the team
Process management	Focusing on content
Outcomes	Problems
Creating rapport and confidence in the relationship – being friendly	Needing to be liked, needing intimacy or affection – needing friendship
Belief in the resourcefulness of the team	Being needed by the team
Eliciting ways forward from the client	Offering ways forward – giving advice
Focusing on the client and their agenda	Focusing on yourself and your agenda
Helping the team attain insight	Offering your own insight as if it is more valuable
Paying attention to your intuition	Believing your intuition is necessarily right and expecting the team to follow it

These things are easy to write and less easy to achieve. This is one reason why coaches need to constantly work at understanding and managing ourselves – we need to be very clear about our core personality, emotional make-up and needs in order to ensure we are not unconsciously intruding these into the coaching process.

Here are some of the other guidelines, tools and techniques that have stood me in good stead for many years.

Managing your physical energy

Firstly, it is imperative to learn to manage your concentration. A team session often lasts all day and sometimes for two or more days. During this time you are probably the only participant who is never allowed to fully switch off at any point. Even during the coffee or lunch break, when others are relaxing, there is generally at least one of the group who wants to have a private word, either to engage in a social, friendly way or to lobby on a point of personal interest. It is important to remember you are *always* on duty, especially if you spend an evening with the group where alcohol is present. Although you may behave in a less formal way during the social aspects of team coaching you are never wholly off duty and never free from the obligation to behave professionally. It is hugely tempting at times to let your guard down and say something inappropriate. I know I made quite a few mistakes of this sort in my early years in the role, getting a little carried away in the social moment.

One skill to develop in terms of managing concentration is to know when to free wheel. No one can be at the peak of concentration for hour after hour: test cricketers who might spend a day or more fielding know they need to switch off between balls. They learn to concentrate only when the ball is in play so they can maintain sharp focus when it really counts. This means developing judgement as to when you can at least partly switch off during a long session. One example of this is when the team is engaged in a structured activity such as an exercise. Assuming you are familiar with the exercise, you can relax your attention for a while, focusing only on any notable behaviour whilst remaining ready to respond if necessary. This is a 'rest' only in the sense that it allows you to throttle back for a short time – you can never switch off fully or it is likely you will miss something important. Even when you are in this relatively freewheeling mode you will probably be thinking ahead to the next stages of the session. Nonetheless it is important to take advantage of any slight relief that may be on offer – even a few minutes of group discussion when it seems they are on track and working well can create a brief respite. Your fullest concentration is needed at moments when your intervention is most vital, such as when the group is losing focus, when there is unhelpful behaviour or when an important process decision needs to be made.

Paying attention to your diet

To maintain energy and concentration it is important to eat and drink properly. Fluctuations in personal energy – for example, through dehydration or low blood sugar – can make it hard to concentrate. Drink plenty of water, avoid the heavy lunch and eat a slow-energy release breakfast such as porridge. The key is to avoid high or low energy 'spikes' and for this reason it is also important to be moderate in the amount of caffeine you ingest.

Changing the scenery

Take whatever chance there is to get a change of environment when you are working in extended sessions. It can be easy to get so wrapped up in a team session that you lose perspective. A brisk walk rather than a portion of pudding after lunch can refresh one's thinking and mood simultaneously: I have frequently thought of a way to develop a session or resolve an issue whilst doing this. If you are staying in a hotel or conference centre to work with your team you will often find them overheated and airless: it is vital to keep your mind alert.

Manage the physical environment to suit your needs: I have become increasingly single-minded about this over the years. Manage the temperature and the lighting to suit how you want to work and to create a physical environment that will help the group to work.

Maintaining confidence

The key emotions you will need to manage well are those that can affect confidence. A confident demeanour is essential if you are to appear credible in your coaching role. This is particularly true at moments of crisis and pressure, when the most important aspect of the role is to convey two key messages: first, that you are in control of yourself, your emotions and your actions; secondly, that you believe in the team and their ability to make progress no matter how difficult the circumstances. I would recommend Paul McKenna's book *Instant Confidence* (McKenna, 2006) for a variety of helpful techniques. The ones I describe here are those I have personally found most helpful.

When the pressure is on I find it useful to manage my physical and emotional state in the following simple ways:

- By breathing – deeply and regularly. Breathing is one of the first aspects of physical functioning to go awry under pressure and steady deep breathing tells your anxious mind that things are under control. What is more, by breathing in this way you are sending a message to the team that you are OK, which they will pick up on, albeit unconsciously.

- Relax muscles and keep centred. This means making sure your muscles stay loose and that you are keeping your centre of gravity low. A tense body with a high centre of gravity – for example, with the weight up in the shoulders – sends a clear message to your brain, and to the group, that things are difficult.
- Listen to your inner voice. Many of us talk to ourselves in our heads and it is useful to pay attention to this voice. I find that under pressure my inner voice sometimes tends to sound anxious and childlike in tone. By adjusting this voice to sound slower, deeper and more resonant I send a confident message to my whole system. If my 'anxious' voice is saying negative things to me, I can choose to say something more positive instead.

Each of these techniques takes mere seconds to put into practice – the key is to pay attention to your personal state so that you can keep it under control before it is too late and loss of confidence takes over.

T-CUP: Thinking Clearly Under Pressure

The mind and body is an interactive system and managing yourself in the ways described above will go a long way to keeping you intellectually focused. However, groups can get themselves tangled up or lost in the discussion process and it is important for the coach to maintain clarity in the face of complex, confusing and pressured situations. Below are some approaches to keep yourself and the group on track.

Focus yourself on the outcome the group is working towards rather than the problems they may perceive in reaching the outcome. Problem-focused thinking absorbs energy and lowers morale, whereas outcome-focused thinking tends to focus energy positively and create a sense of direction. When working with the group on complex issues it can be useful for you and for them to post on a flip chart a visual reminder of what they are trying to achieve. This will also help you to challenge any irrelevant discussion. Summarise the discussion frequently – this is a fairly basic facilitation skill but essential to keep yourself, and the team, on track. If new topics arise in the discussion that threaten to take the central discussion off track make a note of them on flip chart for the team to return to later – this is sometimes called 'car parking'. If the going gets really difficult consider calling a recess – it is amazing how an apparently insoluble issue or situation often seems much simpler or easier after a break.

Summary

Many years ago I worked in a leadership development centre in the Lake District that ran outdoor-based courses. In the grounds of this centre was a ropes course – a series of cunningly devised obstacles constructed amongst the trees that was used to encourage groups to examine and develop their skills in communication, feedback and support. One of the pieces of apparatus was a swinging log: the log was pivoted at one end and supported by a rope on the other so that it would swing from side to side when someone stood on it or moved hastily whilst standing on it. To walk the length of the log required patience and balancing skills. One day I was going round the ropes course myself with another trainer colleague to familiarise myself with the various crux points and to review safety procedures: when it came to the swinging log I repeatedly failed to stay on it. Frustrated with myself, I said I thought the log was just too wobbly to walk along. My colleague asked me just to step back off the log and just look at it. I did so. He then asked me if I could see the log wobbling. I said no. 'So where does the wobble come from?' he asked. Of course, the wobble was not in the log but in *me*. When I learned to stay calm, centred and focused I was able to walk along the log easily – in fact the log became a personal metaphor for self management and I eventually was able to walk along it both forwards and backwards.

The same is true of teams. When the coach or the leader wobbles, so can the team. The heart of effective team management begins with self management. In addition to the self management tips I offer above, lies a longer, lifelong task of understanding oneself and learning to stay in balance when the going gets tough.

Key learning points

- Much of the dynamic that influences team behaviour is cultural and systemic. To work effectively with a team requires some understanding of the wider system of which they are a part.
- It is important for a team coach to recognise when a failing team has passed the point of no return and to be prepared to quit if necessary.
- The heart of effective team coaching and team leadership is being able to understand and manage oneself.

Reflective questions

- Consider the case studies above: what other strategies could the team coach have tried?
- What are your own emotional hot spots? What team or individual behaviours could push you off balance?
- What is your own motivation for wanting to help teams work more effectively?

6   Designing interventions

'Sometimes we need to just do the best we can and then trust in an unfolding we can't design or ordain.'

– Sharon Salzberg

Fixed goals and flexible means – not the other way round – should be the hallmark of your design processes. Team coaching takes a number of forms and one of the most important of these is the designed event aimed at achieving a planned purpose. The design process is emphatically not a science. As in life, things are likely to happen that you cannot predict and you need to be ready for numerous contingencies. As a rule of thumb, no matter what you include in a team day agenda you might aim to bring with you at least twice as much in the way of structured session alternatives – and carry in your head a further range of options in case of the totally unexpected. What was planned as a feedback session may instantly transmute into an emergency planning session due to some unforeseen change in the organisation's circumstances that directly affects the leadership team. You may have to adapt your session and play the facilitator part of the coach's role under such circumstances. You simply must be flexible, tune in to the team and go with the flow – whilst still being prepared to argue at times for doing what you think is right for the team.

Designing a programme of team coaching interventions is a task that needs to be approached carefully. At a minimum the process should:

- Determine the core development agenda for the team through data-gathering exercises and discussion with the team members themselves
- Dovetail both short- and long-term aims for the overall intervention
- Allow frequent input on content and process from team members
- Respond to cultural needs and preferences
- Be sensitive to issues of diversity including those of personality type and learning style
- Remain flexible and willing to change course in terms of aims and processes as the team learns and develops

- Maintain contact and remain responsive to changes in the overall organisation that may affect the team
- Balance the need for support with the need for challenge

Learning styles

There are numerous theories on how people learn best. Without having to subscribe to any particular theory, the team coach should bear in mind that there are different learning preferences and that a variety of media is likely to produce better results – if only by way of stimulating attention – than reliance on just one or two. The most widely known model of learning in the UK is Honey and Mumford's Experiential Learning Theory (Honey and Mumford 1982, 1983). This was developed in the early 1980s and is based on the work of psychologist David Kolb (Kolb and Fry, 1975). The essence of the model is the proposition that there is an optimal mix of learning that includes concrete experience, reviewing the experience, drawing conclusions from the experience, and planning future action on the basis of those conclusions. Many training organisations, particularly those that use a lot of activity-based learning, base their methodology on this model.

The VAK model is also popular. Drawn from Neuro-Linguistic Programming (NLP) the model asserts that some learners benefit most from *visual* (V) sources, such as presentations, slides and videos; some from *auditory* (A) sources, such as lectures and discussions; and others from *kinaesthetic* (K) sources, such as tactile experience or physical activity.

Whilst the team coach does not need to be an expert in these or other models it is important to have a working knowledge and to remember that variety is likely to bring benefit to the design of any team session.

Games and simulations: their merits and dangers

> 'I hear and I forget; I see and I remember; I do and I understand.'
> – *Confucius*

Confucius clearly had his own take on learning styles. Games and simulations can be a powerful way of drawing a team's attention to aspects of the way they work, but can also represent a challenge to the team coach's judgement on what to include in a designed event. On the positive side they can provide a fascinating analogy to the team's processes, inject energy and fun into a team coaching session and create 'breakthrough' insights. They can also highlight areas where the team functions poorly, such as in listening skills, collective planning or problem-solving. Another point of merit is that a vivid exercise experience can provide a memorable reference point for the future. Sometimes a practical exercise can also provide a forum to raise discussion on uncomfortable issues. Used sparingly and with judgement they can be one of the most effective resources available to the team coach. However, some team members may view them with suspicion. Some will have had experience of team-building events in which the games or activities employed seemed trivial or pointless; or worse, actively damaging to team spirit. Activities designed to provide 'fun' can be fraught with pitfalls, and the legacy of their misuse has hindered the reputation of serious team development over the years.

Activities to avoid are of the 'paintballing' kind, ostensibly designed to create something mysterious called 'bonding', which many sceptics consider pointless and intrinsically artificial. Some people find such exercises fun and energising, but many find them silly and embarrassing – or worse, stressful. They are often not facilitated, have at best fuzzy outcomes and are notoriously prone to mishap. At best they can provide a pleasant common experience, allowing team members to relax and perhaps get to know each other better: at worst they can be divisive, cater for the real interests of only some of the team and provoke disagreements and upsets – without providing for how any such upsets are going to be resolved.

Team development is about much more than allowing the team to let its hair down. If an exercise does not help a team to develop knowledge, skill, learning capability or confidence then it has no real place in team coaching. Certainly, exercises and events that are purely macho in nature should be reserved for a very small minority of teams, and employed only after rigorous thought by all concerned.

Some years ago there was a notorious TV programme featuring an exponent of such overtly 'macho' events that set the reputation of more serious and reputable outdoor management and leadership centres back for years. In this programme the event leader would stand on crags in his vest and shorts and shout provocations at the participants. He would frequently surprise them by suddenly changing the nature or rules of a particular task so they became faced with a bigger or more daunting challenge at short notice – essentially tricking them and betraying their initial trust. No consideration at all appeared to be given to individual needs and the only lessons offered were the ones the course leader felt were worthwhile. He operated entirely from his own value set and openly despised any contradictions to his views. He employed a group of young, fit outdoors instructors as 'tutors' who could have had little experience of the real world of work from which the participants came. Perhaps the key image of the programme was that of an unfit middle-aged senior executive gasping for breath as he attempted to scale a steep Scottish mountain with a twenty-something instructor barking abuse at him. This kind of event is fine for individuals who want to stretch themselves on a voluntary basis but has little relevance to team development in the real world of organisational life.

Always consider whether the given activity is suitable for all the team members. Due thought and attention needs to be given to questions such as:

- Is everyone physically capable of taking part in the exercise?
- Are there any aspects of the exercise that could disadvantage any part of the group?
- Are there any cultural sensitivities or preferences that need to be taken into account?
- Are there any language issues in the group that make the exercise more complicated for some members than others?

At the very least, the team coach should consider whether this exercise can be reasonably offered to virtually anyone who is able to come to work. Even the exercises I describe here need to be used only in the right context and with a specific learning outcome in mind.

There is a very large selection of team development games available. Some are elaborate and extremely expensive to buy. Others are easy to set up and cost little or nothing to run, and I describe a small selection of the latter in Chapter 8. As far as I am aware there is no copyright on these games (unless otherwise indicated) and from my point of view you are certainly free to use them. The very useful www.businessballs.com website also provides plenty of free activities.

From long and hard experience I have found it important to be absolutely familiar with each and every exercise, including:

- What the technical solutions or answers might be to any given exercise – some teams get quite cross if you as the coach do not know how an exercise is supposed to work
- What to expect in terms of how different teams might respond, especially if they struggle to succeed
- How some individuals may choose to react to particular exercises
- How to adapt the exercises to different circumstances – to allow for restrictions on time or space, for example
- How to judge the appropriate level of challenge for any given team
- How to explain the justification and benefits of any given exercise

I would far rather have a small handful of 'bomb-proof' exercises with which I am thoroughly familiar and have full confidence than have a huge repertoire for its own sake. The exercises I offer here have been road tested for many years and if used properly are robust.

Icebreakers and introductory exercises

There are many books and manuals offering ice-breaker ideas and other games and simulations. They need to be approached with caution, as their misuse can do more harm than good. All the exercises and tools I introduce are ones I have used personally for many years and I have confidence in them if they are used as described here. Although you can never guarantee outcomes, you can certainly improve your chances by planning carefully on the basis of experience.

For some team participants, icebreakers can evoke fear of exposure and embarrassment. Much depends on how well the team members know each other already and on the overall climate and culture of the team and the organisation of which it is part. A poorly selected icebreaker can jeopardise the success of a whole session or fatally undermine the credibility of the team coach or leader. I am not a fan of icebreakers for their own sake and prefer any activity to come with a purpose that has face validity for team members in terms of the overall goals they are working towards. Team members should not have to ask, 'What is the point of this exercise?'

I introduce one icebreaker below that I have found useful with newly founded teams but which can also be of value to those that have been together for some time – it can be amazing how little people know about each other even when they have worked together for years.

The 'Coat of Arms' Exercise

This can be a great way of helping team members to learn more about each other in a non-threatening way. It is particularly useful early in a team coaching assignment when a new team is coming together – or if two established teams have been combined. The steps are as follows:

- Ask the team what it would be good to know about each other as individuals. Jot down the answers on a flip chart. (Typical items include: background, education, career, family, personal values, hobbies, achievements, fears, wishes, sporting or musical interests.)
- Ask each person to draw a personal coat of arms using flip chart paper and felt tip pens and any other creative materials available. Get them to include words, pictures or symbols that encapsulate the information they wish to share. Explain that it is up to them what they choose to divulge.
- When each person has finished writing or drawing (usually after about ten minutes), ask each person in turn to stand up and talk about their coat of arms for a few minutes.
- After each person has spoken, ask the group if there is anything else they would like to ask of the speaker in addition to what they have said – invite questions.
- Get the group to put their coat of arms up on the wall, using Blu Tack® or similar, so they can be looked at and referred to throughout the programme.

This exercise can be used easily by either a team coach or a team leader. It is a gentle way of building interpersonal knowledge. People often reveal unexpected achievements, interests or key events in their lives. The key to success is to emphasise that this is not an art competition. Some team members are reluctant to do anything that smacks of creativity so it is important to emphasise that it is the information that counts, not the drawing. It is also important to emphasise that they need only include information they are comfortable talking about: individuals have very different views about their own privacy and it is counter-productive to allow any kind of pressure on people to reveal more than they want to.

All exercises can throw up surprises. I ran this exercise once with a media team whose boss had a reputation as something of a tough nut. I had described the programme I planned to run for one of his team days and he said he was not very keen to participate as he did not want the team learning anything about him that might make him seem weak. I encouraged him to participate, and sure enough one of the categories that came up for sharing was that of 'weaknesses'. The boss plunged in and revealed that from an early age he had been irrationally terrified of being eaten by fish! The group did not initially know how to respond, but ultimately a sense of wicked humour broke in: for the rest of the event any possible means of referring to fish and their potential for inflicting harm was seized upon. Luckily the tough-guy boss also had a sense of humour and took it all in good part – in fact the joke broke the ice and had the positive effect of humanising him.

One point of detail: as team coach it can be useful to complete and talk about your own coat of arms – otherwise it can be seen as something you are doing *to* the team. On the other hand, if you do decide to do the exercise yourself it is important not to grab the limelight by talking too much or revealing a string of sensational aspects of your own life that distract the team from learning about each other – do not play the star.

Models to help a team think and learn

A team can benefit from its members becoming more aware of each other as individuals with different experiences and abilities, and of the team as an entity with its habitual ways of working. Often a team also needs to find ways of taking a fresh look at an old problem or of meeting a new challenge. Here are some models that can be extremely helpful in refreshing a team's thinking.

De Bono's Six Thinking Hats

This is an excellent model for helping a team to think more flexibly and is an excellent tool for facilitation of tricky or complex subjects such as strategy formulation, or for addressing particularly intractable problems. Edward de Bono is a renowned creative thinker who is often credited with the invention of 'lateral' thinking. The basic premise that he explores in his 'thinking hats' model is the idea, drawn from the commonplace phrase 'put on your thinking hat', that it would be useful if we had more than one type of thinking hat to put on. He devised a model of six distinctly different thinking styles that a team might usefully employ, as in the table below. The idea is that in looking at a tough or complex issue the team would expand its thinking by exploring the issue from each of these styles.

White Hat	Red Hat
This hat is about facts and about assumptions about facts. The team will wear this hat when it is sharing knowledge and checking that everyone is in possession of the same information. It is particularly useful for checking that everyone in a team is working from the same factual assumptions. The dialogue associated with this hat is cool, dispassionate and non-judgemental.	This hat is about emotion and intuition. Wearing this hat, a team allows itself to express emotion legitimately, as opposed to keeping it buried for fear that it is dangerous or inappropriate. This hat also allows the team to work with hunches or 'gut feeling', allowing the open discussion of thoughts which may not have immediate rational explanation. The dialogue associated with this hat is openly emotional.
Black Hat	**Green Hat**
This hat is about critical thinking and looking at potential downsides and flaws in proposals and ideas the group may be considering. This is a hat that can be over-used and can stifle creativity in teams, because it is safe and conservative – even sceptical. However, it is still a legitimate hat when used moderately. The dialogue associated with this hat is coldly logical. The word 'but' will feature heavily.	This hat is about open creativity – the 'thinking outside the box' hat. This is the hat a team can use when it is bogged down or going round in circles or when it simply needs fresh ideas and approaches. Using this hat, a team can brainstorm, play games or use other creative exercises without invoking 'black hat' thinking. The dialogue associated with this hat is enthusiastic and playful.
Yellow Hat	**Blue Hat**
This hat is about optimism and vision. The team can wear this hat when engaging in strategic thinking or in creating a new strategy. It can also be useful in shifting a team from 'problem focused' thinking to 'outcome focused' thinking. Sometimes when a team is bogged down in problem-solving it may need to wear this hat for a fresh injection of energy. The dialogue associated with this hat is open and hopeful.	This hat is about process monitoring and evaluation of how the team is working and behaving. A team coach or facilitator may wear this hat for the team quite a lot of the time: but sometimes it is important for the team to do their own review and reflection on how they are working. It is a useful hat for the team to wear to review the quality of thinking and of behaviour within the team. The dialogue associated with this hat is dispassionate and objective.

1 Follow this procedure: Introduce the model to the team and check their understanding.

2 Spend some time refining the issue to be discussed, ensuring there are clear *outcomes* for the discussion – for example, is the team looking for ideas or decisions?

3 Write on a flip chart the topic for discussion and the desired outcomes to ensure there is a clear focus.

4 Ask the team to wear only *one* hat at a time. For example, if the team is wearing the yellow hat it is not permitted for team members to offer black hat objections.

5 It is generally useful for the team to begin with the white hat in order that each member starts from much the same point of information and understanding. Then work around the hats, noting down key points of the discussion. If the discussion becomes blocked in any way introduce the blue hat so that the team can review its progress and behaviour.

6 Finish with a review of learning and an encapsulation of the action points.

This exercise is only fully powerful if the team commits to the discipline of wearing one hat at a time. I have used this exercise frequently over the years and have found it useful in helping a team to think and talk more resourcefully. I have been struck with how over-used the black hat is in management culture – and how resistant managers can be to adopting anything other than a critical, sceptical style. As a team coach and facilitator I have sometimes had to work hard to legitimise the adoption of any other style even for short periods but sometimes it has had real breakthrough value to do so. One team I have coached for several years found the model so liberating it has become part of their vocabulary for everyday business.

It is worth noting that where the climate of trust in a team is relatively low the prospect of working in the 'red hat' zone can become more charged with anxiety and tension, with some possibility of emotional upset or outburst. Whilst this needs a degree of attention and care from the coach, it is important for the team coach to let the team do what it needs to do. They are adults, after all, and the coaching role is one of partnership rather than of parenting. A good working contract with the team (see below) should give you permission to intervene if necessary in any potentially damaging interaction, but it is important to let the team work to resolve its own issues. I have seen many teams benefit from a spell of letting off steam and perhaps surfacing long-held difficult feelings. Like many aspects of the team coaching role, it is a matter of fine judgement. No coach should want to see emotional disruption or damaging behaviour, but a healthy airing of frustration or discontent can pave the way for the team to move to a closer understanding and, ultimately, even a higher level of trust.

Action learning

Action learning was a technique pioneered in the 1940s in the UK by Professor Reg Revans whilst he was director of education at the National Coal Board between 1945 and 1950 (Revans, 1983). Revans can claim to be one of the fathers of the methodology of team coaching as he pioneered a 'non-expert' approach to team learning and problem-solving in which structured questioning and reflection techniques were used to help individuals bring fresh thinking to their issues and problems. He was actually opposed to the use of specialist coaches or team facilitators, believing a team could work on its own issues, but his techniques and ideas have been extensively revised and adopted to create a variety of methodologies which can sit under the banner of action learning. The key is in the name: action learning. Revans and his followers believed that powerful learning does not take place without accompanying action and that action should not happen without learning.

The core of the method can be described as follows:

- A team will meet at regular intervals for half a day or a full day to learn from the real-life problems and issues they face and to create new action for dealing with the issues from their learning. A popular and pragmatic approach to this is to begin the work in learning sets with a team coach and gradually to transfer management of the sets to the team itself.
- During the sets, individual members of the team will describe a real-life issue where they feel the need for fresh thinking and learning, taking turns to speak. They will describe the problem as they currently see it.
- The other members of the team will ask questions and offer thoughts on the problem and on how the 'owner' of the problem is seeing it.
- Alternatively or additionally the issue owner may sit out for a while and simply listen whilst the rest of the group discusses the issue.
- The issue owner reflects on his or her learning from these discussions.
- The issue owner will then decide on the action he or she is going to take.
- At the next session the issue owner reports back on the results of the action and their reflections on the whole process.

This process is conditional on the team contracting for the behaviour needed to produce an effective learning environment – for example, agreeing not to interrupt, to offer constructive feedback, and so on.

Life story sharing

This is a great exercise for teams whose members share a sense of commitment and are up for the challenge of building a real sense of togetherness. The essence of the exercise is listening and learning. It is a highly personal thing to tell a group of people something of your life story and therefore even broaching the exercise is a judgement call for the team coach or leader. I use this exercise sparingly, when I sense a team is ready to go the next step in rapport-building and where I believe there are no individuals in the team likely to feel stressed by the experience. As with the coat of arms exercise what people choose to reveal is entirely down to them. The steps are very simple:

- Gain agreement that the team will undertake the exercise, emphasising the right of any individuals to keep to themselves anything they do not want to divulge.
- Explain that the aim is for each individual to tell their individual life story in whatever way they choose but within a five minute time limit so that the exercise does not take too long.
- Give perhaps ten or fifteen minutes of quiet reflection time for individuals to prepare their stories.
- Individuals tell their stories in turn, with an opportunity at the end of each story for members of the group to ask questions.
- At the end, review the exercise in terms of learning and value for the team.

Over the years I have found the response to the exercise remarkably consistent. Sometimes there is apprehension at the beginning. By the end what generally happens is that the team grows in respect for itself. The stories that people have to tell often contain remarkable achievements and also great challenges that they have overcome. Learning what has gone into their colleague's lives can also help to bring insight into what drives individual behaviour. This is not an exercise for the faint hearted but can have extremely positive benefits.

Review techniques

Every team coach needs a range of review techniques. At the very least it is important to build up a range of good review questions. You can get a lot of mileage out of reviewing team exercises or discussions with a set of questions such as:

- What did we do well?
- What was not so good?

- How could we improve what we are doing?
- How well are we communicating/planning/involving people?
- What is hindering us?
- How should we address this?

From time to time more structured and in-depth reviews may be necessary, such as when a team has been through a tough time or finished an important project. Designing review techniques can be a source of fun and creativity for the coach and can add depth and intensity to a team event. Below is a selection of road-tested techniques.

The wall of well-being

This is a deceptively simple technique that can be surprisingly powerful in bringing to light important issues for a team. The aim is for each person in turn to describe their experience of working in the team and for the team to compare, and then learn from, individual experiences.

To begin with, create a wall chart. This can be drawn on an existing white board or on three sheets of flip chart paper (portrait) taped together to form a screen. Draw a horizontal and a vertical axis, as for a simple line graph. The horizontal axis represents time, and can be calibrated according to the length of past time the team feels it is useful to review. I have generally found that about six months is the maximum, and sometimes as little as a week or month is enough, particularly if the team is emerging from a particularly intense period of work or has recently experienced some kind of traumatic event. The vertical axis represents well-being or morale. The middle of the vertical line represents an individual's 'normal' or average level of well-being. The top of the line represents maximum possible well-being and the bottom of the line the lowest possible level.

Explain that the purpose of the exercise is to learn about how individuals have experienced the agreed period of time with a view to learning lessons from which the whole team can benefit. Give the team five or ten minutes of reflection time in which they can privately review their experience of the period of time the team is going to look at. Ask for a volunteer to go first and ask them to draw a line that represents their well-being over the period. Ask them to explain as they go. If they experience a 'high', where the line goes near to the top of the page, then ask them to say something about what went into creating that high; if it is a low, what went into creating that low. The aim is for them to tell the story of the period. Ask the team just to listen until the individual story is over, which normally takes two or three minutes, before asking questions. As the stories unfold, write up on a flip chart the things that are described as enhancing or reducing well-being, in a table form. You can keep it relatively short by adding an asterisk to repeated items rather than writing them out again in full. The lists might look something like this, only longer:

Plus factors	Minus factors
Sense of achievement***	Exhaustion from overwork*
Positive feedback from boss*	Argument with colleague**
Felt supported by colleagues	Negative feedback from customer
And so on	And so on

When everyone is finished, look at the overall chart and ask questions like: 'What surprises are there? Did we know how down a certain person felt? How do we respond to the idea that what raises some people's morale (such as an intense challenge) can have the opposite effect on others in the team? What have we learned about each other? How can we support each other better going forward?

This exercise can have surprisingly powerful results. I once ran it for a media team who were initially sceptical about its worth, but once they got started it occupied about three quarters of the day. Sometimes it can provide a forum for individuals to say something important about issues they cared about that might not have had legitimacy in any other context. Deep feelings can be evoked. One of the most powerful realisations is often that what seems obviously motivating to one or more members of the team may be having a diametrically opposite effect on others.

In general I have found that the whole process tends to take up to an hour. You can use the list of plus and minus factors as a springboard to discussion on how the team can improve morale in general, or how individuals might be better supported.

The 0–10 scale

Using simple scales is one of the easiest ways of reviewing. A scale can be used flexibly to review specific exercises, facilitated discussions or team performance across a range of dimensions. The coach simply has to ask the right question in relation to the scale. Examples are: 'On a scale of 0–10 how do we rate . . .

- Our performance in the exercise?
- Our satisfaction with this discussion?
- How well we support each other?
- The level of creativity in the team?
- Our sense of mutual trust?'

Whatever the question, the coach asks each person to write down their score. This prevents individuals from being influenced by the scores offered by others in the team. The coach then asks each person to reveal their score. The ensuing discussion can be about variations in the score that reflect a range of individual judgements, about surprises, or about developing understanding of why individuals scored as they did.

Feelings reviews

Teams are not always comfortable talking about feelings but sometimes it is really important that they do. One simple review technique is to ask each member of the team to write down a single word representing how they feel in a particular moment – for example, following an exercise or an important discussion. Each person speaks their chosen word in turn and then a discussion can be held to build understanding of the various emotional states expressed. This method ensures some input from every member of the team without putting anyone on the spot.

Agenda gathering

Agenda gathering typically happens before a team event and can take the form of structured interviews, telephone discussions or an email invitation to contribute ideas and views for the event. Sometimes, though, the team may need to create an agenda on the spot. The coach needs a way of creating a valid and focused agenda that represents the needs of the whole team. If the issues are numerous and complex, this can create a challenge. An elegant way of achieving a clear and focused agenda is an exercise using Post-it® notes sometimes referred to as the Democracy Wall.

The democracy wall

Having established the need for the team to build a working agenda around a number of issues you will need a short time – for example, a quick refreshment break – to prepare. Alternatively, get the team to help with the practicalities. Here are the steps:

- Create a large screen made of three sheets of flip chart paper, attached to a wall with Blu Tack® or masking tape.
- Distribute something like fifty Post-it® notes to the team, with an equal number for each person (if there are ten in the team they get five each, if eight in the team, six each. The point is that more than about fifty notes becomes unwieldy).
- Give each person a felt-tip pen. Ask them to write a *headline* of just a few words on each note, each headline representing a topic they wish to discuss.

- As the team is writing headlines, pick up completed Post-its® and begin to place them on the screen, looking for headline items that seem to have connection with each other and grouping them together.
- When all the Post-its® have been written, complete placing them on the wall in what you take to be groups of associated topics.
- Invite the team to stand with you in front of the screen. Ask for their comments on the way the topics have been grouped and make the adjustments they suggest.
- Ask the team to label each group with an overall title. Draw a circle round the group and label it with its title.
- Finally, ask the team to decide the order of priority for discussion of the groups: normally they will be chosen in order of size, the group with the largest number of Post-its® coming first, and so on.

Normally this will result in six to eight topics, each with subheadings, prioritised as to importance – in fact, an agenda. Not only will everyone have had equal involvement in its creation, but the process itself will stimulate team discussion.

Interventions for informal contracting

Contracting can be divided into two stages. The formal stage covers when, how often and where the team will meet and what it agrees to work on. The informal stage addresses how the team agrees to behave. I have found two methods of contracting for behaviour that work well. One of these, based on visioning success, is described in Chapter 2. The 'gallery' technique is a useful alternative.

Contracting questions gallery

This is a good way of involving all members of a team in creating a contract for attitudes and behaviours. Give each person half a sheet of flip chart paper and a pen and ask them to write their answers to the following questions:

- What do I want from this team development process?
- How do I need to think and behave in order to help get what I want?
- How do others in the team need to think and behave?
- What is the most important behaviour we need to adopt to be successful?
- How could we sabotage ourselves?
- How can we ensure we do not sabotage ourselves?

Give each person some time to reflect and ask them to put their answers on their piece of paper. When they have finished, ask them to put their names on the paper and Blu Tack® it to the wall. When all the papers are on the wall, ask the team members to walk around and look at the answers given by their colleagues. Hold a brief discussion on the key themes and ask for commitment to the key behaviours.

The team charter

As part of the process of developing a team you will frequently find they need to agree a core set of principles and practices for how they will work together back in the workplace. One way of creating this is to suggest they write a team charter. Divide the team into three groups and ask each group to work separately on creating a list of the top five things the team needs to do to work together effectively; about twenty minutes should be enough. When the three groups come back together, ask each group to describe its five success criteria and discuss them with their colleagues. There is usually a great deal of overlap in what each group submits. Then, in discussion with the whole team, write up a definitive list drawn from the three lists, and ask the team to commit to this final list as a team charter. You may even ask each person to sign the list in felt tip pen: this adds a bit of drama, and the symbolism of having signed in public makes it very hard for someone to renege in future. Ask the team to look after the charter: some teams make laminated copies and give them out to team members. This is a simple but powerful process and can be an important part of team development.

Managing feedback in teams

It is important to be able to facilitate sessions where team members can offer useful feedback. Feedback is essential to personal learning – but can be tricky to manage because few people welcome any feedback that can be felt as criticism. As a precursor to any feedback session it is important to check that the team has a shared view of what feedback really is and what are its key constituents. The coach can help the team distinguish between feedback and criticism, as follows:

Feedback	Criticism
Information designed to allow the recipient to make informed choices	A dumping of judgemental feelings and thoughts
Describes specific behaviours	Is general and sometimes personal
Is a two-way conversation	Is a one-way dumping process
Identifies a way forward	Is blaming and focused only on the past
Is timely	Is either too soon after the event or so long after that it loses impact
Is descriptive not judgemental	Is blaming
Is 'owned' by the feedback giver	Is attributed to others and what 'they' think

Feedback can be ad hoc, but sometimes it is useful to offer a structured approach. If doing this, it is generally best to avoid the 'spotlight' technique in which each person in the team is given a turn to listen to the views of the rest of the team. This is simply too stressful for some people and in any case depends for any success on everyone in the team skilfully and conscientiously applying the rules outlined above.

One useful formula is the 'feedback carousel'. In this formula, the team stands up and moves around. Each person spends two minutes with each of their colleagues. In this time they take it in turns to offer two bits of feedback, based on the following sentences:

'One thing about the way you work as a colleague I really appreciate is . . .'

'I would also appreciate . . .'

You can adjust the precise nature of these sentences as appropriate. The virtue of the technique is that it tends to focus on key messages and does not get bogged down in too much analysis. It is also a good energy builder.

Summary

Designing team events is an area of creativity for the team coach or leader. One of the great satisfactions is developing the creativity to adapt sessions according to circumstances or to create something new at short notice. A team session should offer impact, stimulus and, ideally, good memories for the team. Remember, it is not a science. Flexibility is needed to ensure that every session meets the mark. You need to be prepared to revise plans or even abandon them as the occasion demands.

Learning points

- All design needs to recognise learning style, personality mix, cultural nuances and the practical circumstances facing the team.
- You can rarely come too well prepared – you should allow for at least some of your carefully designed sessions to be abandoned and be prepared to offer something else as circumstances dictate.
- Your design should allow and encourage full participation from everyone.
- The more you involve the team in your design process the more they will respond positively, but you should keep a surprise or two up your sleeve in order to keep energy and attention high.

Reflective questions

- How clear are you about your own learning style, personality type or cultural assumptions?
- When you were part of a team learning event yourself, what were the best and most powerful parts of the experience?
- What kinds of ingredients might you be tempted to favour or avoid, and why?
- What might be your personal development areas in the role of designer?

7 The impact of organisational culture

'There is no such thing as society: there are individual men and women, and there are families.'

– Margaret Thatcher

The team is not a hermetically sealed object but an entity of almost entirely porous nature, subject to and part of a complex web of cultural and systemic influences. Much of the 'internal' team dynamic is in fact created outside of the 'walls' of the team and is a product of social, organisational and cultural forces, which the team members themselves may be only partly aware of.

All teams are subject to influences from the wider organisational and social systems in which they operate. Some important influences are simple but easily overlooked factors such as:

- *Team size.* This is hugely important. Is the team actually of the right size to benefit from being able to learn from its own interaction? In my experience anything larger than ten makes it hard for a team to function as a learning unit.
- *Longevity.* Does the team last for long enough to create a real sense of common commitment and purpose amongst its members or does its ephemeral nature mean most interaction is purely transactional?
- *Proximity.* Does the team work with enough physical closeness to engender a sense of togetherness, including the all-important informal contact that provides social glue?
- *Capacity.* Has the team really got the resources in terms of time, experience, knowledge and skill to be successful, and to benefit from learning opportunities?

More broadly, the team is influenced by the embracing organisational culture merely by being a part of it.

At its simplest, organisational culture can be defined as 'the way it is around here' – the default view of what an organisation should be like. We tend to assume that the way things are done in our own culture is somehow the 'right' way, just as peoples have traditionally considered their own country as the centre of the world, the Chinese calling China 'The Middle Kingdom' and the ancient Scandinavians using a similar name for theirs – 'Midgaard' (Hofstede and Hofstede 2005).

In analysing a culture it is useful to make a distinction between what is visible and what is deep and often hidden. In the context of work, the *visible* signs of culture include:

- How people dress – including the level of formality or informality
- Décor and furnishings
- Physical layout – for example, offices or open plan working
- Dining or refreshment facilities
- Use or otherwise of visible logos and symbols

I once encountered a manager whose contention was that you can tell everything you need to know about an organisation by the state of the toilets.

Deep aspects of culture are more subtly expressed and will take longer to assess, but will still connect strongly with the visible signs. Deep culture includes:

- Core values – both official and espoused – and those unofficial values that are expressed in actual behaviour (sometimes very different)
- Beliefs – the mental models and assumptions that underpin the culture – the default view of how it is, or should be
- Core identity – the core sense of self that is a combination of all the above factors within the surrounding environment and broader social culture

Exercises that address whole organisational systems

Open space events

These were originally developed in America. Legend has it that they are rooted in feedback from conventional conferences which judged that the most enjoyable and rewarding parts were the coffee breaks. This created the idea that an event organised on the principle of one long coffee break might prove valuable. This led to the development of a highly flexible format in which numbers from about twelve to five hundred could take part. Essentially the events are organised around a single big issue or question. Anyone who has a stake in the issue, be they directly or indirectly involved, can be invited. The participants gather in a space in which they can work flexibly. Refreshments, relaxation areas and flip charts are supplied. Early in the event a facilitator will ask people what specific interests or topics they wish to discuss within the 'big' issue, and these topics are logged on a central wall so people can see which discussions are available. From that point on, participants choose which discussions to join and for how long. All ideas are written down and taken away. After the event everyone gets a copy of all the written materials so they have a record of what has been discussed in other groups.

These events are suitable for use by larger teams, or for teams who want to actively involve stakeholders, such as colleagues from connected teams, customers or other interest groups – teams, in other words, who want to engage with the whole system.

Experience of running these events has taught me:

- They can be very valuable at putting parts of a system into direct, face-to-face contact with each other. Frequently there are animated discussions between people who may previously have only communicated by email.
- They build networks and enhance trust and understanding between different parts of a system.
- Some leaders or managers often have fears that the events will be anarchic and need reassurance in advance that this will not be the case. In practice participants almost invariably put in maximum effort and are generally involved far more than they could be in conventional event formats involving large numbers.
- As there are normally lots of ideas and proposals generated in the discussions, leaders need to be primed to respond to these ideas and to send clear signals in advance, and again on the day, as to how they will do this so that participants have clear expectations. One practice I have found to be effective in relatively small open space events (say up to twenty participants) is for the leaders to conduct an active review of the output in the last hour, giving a preliminary indication of which proposals or ideas are a) immediately acceptable and actionable, b) worthy of further consideration or c) impractical or undesirable – a kind of 'traffic light' system.
- Managerial response to the output of ideas and suggestions then has to be rapid and full. I have seen events attended by fifty to a hundred people that have generated about the same number of active proposals and ideas. There is nothing worse than this upsurge of energy and voluntary contribution foundering and dissipating. I have tended to coach the leadership team fairly intensively on this issue before embarking on any open-space style project. They have to realise that the ensuing output cannot be dealt with adequately by adopting a 'business as usual' approach.

Stakeholder analysis exercises

These are particularly useful for teams that are engaged in strategic planning and need to root their thinking in a whole-system perspective. If time or resources do not allow the team to conduct extensive discussions or surveys with their stakeholders, or if the team just needs to do some 'quick and dirty' thinking, they can use the following exercise, which the coach can set up and help them to run:

- First list all the relevant stakeholders of the team, including team members themselves, customers of the team, colleagues in other departments or teams, senior managers in the organisation, external interest groups.
- Allocate one or two members of the team to represent each stakeholder group: some flexibility may be required here – for example if team numbers are small, each sub-group may need to tackle more than one stakeholder grouping.
- The sub-groups then work separately: each imagines it is part of their allocated stakeholder group and addresses key questions, such as 'What does this stakeholder group most expect/need/want from the team? What does this say about our strategic direction and the way we need to perform?'
- When this exercise in empathy is finished, the results can be compared and fed into the team's thinking and decision-making.

The 'Supply Chain' exercise

This is an excellent exercise developed by a former colleague of mine (please see references and contact details in Chapter 8). The exercise illustrates how individual and team behaviour are fundamentally affected by the structural dynamics of organisations. It is a great piece of equipment for the team coach. The exercise materials consist of:

- A number of thin, coloured nylon ropes
- Belts on which are a number of loops for fixing the ropes and for holding plastic links
- A large jar of coloured plastic links
- A set of cards that illustrate patterns of coloured links in specific sequences

Each participant puts on a belt. They are then linked together in a set structure using the ropes. Each person gets a card which represents their individual target for acquiring a set pattern of coloured links. The coach then randomly distributes the exact number of links that represents the sum of the individual targets so that everyone has links in their possession but not the ones they individually need. Following a set of clear rules the group then attempts to pass the links round the system in such a way that everyone gets the links they need. What this means is that for the team to succeed it has to behave in a whole-system way. If individuals go for their personal targets at the expense of others the system gets clogged and the team fails.

What almost invariably happens is that individuals only communicate with those to whom they are directly linked. Small subgroups tend to talk and work together, ignoring those who are at distant points on the chain. Those who are connected to numerous other individuals or who form conduits between subgroups often become over-burdened with communication duties or just become blocks in the system.

The coach can set up the system in all sorts of ways to produce different behaviours and results. What frequently surprises participants is the degree to which it is the system itself that produces a lot of the behaviours. The exercise can then be reviewed to look at systems issues that affect performance within the team or within the wider organisational setting.

The role of language in team culture

It is easy to overlook language as an important factor in defining – and developing – team culture. We tend to take language in our own teams and social groups pretty much for granted. Language is in fact both a reflection of culture and a means of transforming it.

As *reflectors* of culture the similes and metaphors we use express the way we view our world, ourselves and the relationships between the two. Organisations routinely develop their own modes of expression – the way they talk about things – and teams within organisations do the same. Paying attention to how they express themselves and describe things in words is often the fast route to understanding their overall mental models about the organisation or team they work in. The metaphors they employ can reveal what is both good and bad about the culture they inhabit and create.

Some years ago I was working with a management team in the UK civil aerospace industry. During a discussion I was facilitating on strategy, one of the executives piped up, 'The battle for supremacy of the air is going to be fought over the Pacific Rim!' Phrases like 'We need to send our best men over the top – send in the big guns', 'We'll have to hit them hard' and 'There are going to be casualties' poured forth, fundamentally colouring the tone of the discussion. The dominant metaphor was clearly 'business as war', and there was no doubt the team saw themselves as warriors or soldiers fighting a business battle.

In a media organisation I worked in, the metaphors at the top of the organisation changed almost overnight as a new chief executive took charge. Whereas the previous incumbent's 'reign' had generated metaphors associated with public service, entertainment and show business, the new language of senior management was much more to do with hard, machine-like efficiency and organisational effectiveness. The language was so loaded with management consultancy jargon that a nationally famous satirical magazine devoted a weekly column to reporting on and ridiculing the language used in internal memos and papers. Meanwhile the rank and file in the organisation, most of whom were shocked at the abrupt change of tone, created their own metaphors to describe the new regime. One group of senior journalists I worked with described the accession of the new regime as 'year zero' – a reference to the tyranny of Pol Pot in Cambodia, reflecting their outraged sense that the previous, much-cherished culture had simply been cast aside. At internal meetings and conferences featuring senior managers, many staff took to playing what they called 'bullshit bingo' – each had a card laden with popular 'management speak' terms, which they would tick off as they were uttered from the platform or head of the table. Many a conference audience would erupt into gales of laughter as a speaker was interrupted by a gleeful bellow of 'house!' from the audience.

In another media organisation in which I was coaching the senior team, whilst they were discussing their strengths and weaknesses, they came to discuss the idea of the team as a 'family'. Some of the team enthusiastically grasped this metaphor, talking positively about the sense of warmth, support and belonging they experienced in the team. As the conversation proceeded, they began to extend the metaphor, talking about who represented whom in the metaphorical family. This created some amusement and discomfort as one of the team was described as the 'mad uncle' – someone whose presence and contributions was seen as somewhat detached and eccentric.

There are a number of core metaphors that seem to recur frequently in organisational life, each with implied strengths and weaknesses for how the organisation or team within it sees itself and functions. See Figure 7.1 for some common examples. In addition you may encounter numerous other kinds of metaphor, such as *theatrical* ('the show must go on', staff as 'performers', 'front of house' and 'back of house') or *medieval court* ('they are the robber barons of the organisation', 'this is my fiefdom').

Gareth Morgan (Morgan, 2006) has written about the organisation as 'psychic prison' where only certain types of behaviour or speech, or even attitude, are acceptable. Most organisations have at least *some* 'psychic prison' in their make-up. A striking example was one management team in the hospitality industry where the constant mantra was about 'growing and nurturing our people' but where any kind of complaint or unhappiness was ruthlessly punished, usually by posting the complainant to an unpopular location or by blocking their promotion hopes.

Metaphor: organisation as . . .	Sample phrases and words	Potential positives	Potential weaknesses
Military/war	'Over the top', 'Casualties', 'Blood on the walls', 'Send in the big guns'	Purposeful, focused, dynamic	Inflexible, harsh culture, people sacrificed, ethical issues
Machine	'Well-oiled machine', 'Spanner in the works', 'Keep the wheels turning'	Efficiency, reliability, certainty	Inflexible, lack of creativity, people seen as commodities
Game	'Another throw of the dice', 'Let's play our trump card'	Fun, energised, creative, competitive	Lack of goal focus, trivialising of serious issues
Family	'We're just one big happy family here', 'keep it in the family'	Loyalty, warmth, commitment, support	Cloning – recruiting people who fit in, scapegoating of the 'black sheep' of the family, lack of objective fairness in management
Organism	'We've planted the seeds of recovery', 'Clear away the dead wood', 'We grow our people'	Emphasis on growth, nurturing, development	Potential chaos – lack of control, growth coming too quickly to sustain the culture
Elite sports team	'Don't drop the ball', 'We need to score here', 'It's game day'	Discipline, high performance, achievement focus	There are many different types of team, each with very different structures and disciplines – what works for one context may be unsuitable for others

Figure 7.1 Common metaphors of organisational life

Language not only reflects culture, it also creates and reinforces it. Helping teams to become more aware of the language they use and its significance in reinforcing culture is a powerful means of helping teams – especially leadership teams – to learn and develop.

Numerous coaches have experienced impressive results in helping teams to understand and develop their own culture using the following simple exercise.

The simile exercise

This is particularly useful with a team that is still at the early stage of working out its own sense of strengths and weaknesses – and may also be beginning to think about development targets and performance improvement. Be aware it may attract a degree of scepticism initially from some teams – but almost invariably a team will have a crack at it after a little bit of coaxing. The results have been very positive in terms of team learning and focus on what they have to do to develop.

Step 1: Divide the team into small groups of about three.

Step 2: Ask each trio to create three or four similes that describe aspects of their current experience of working in the team, using the formula: 'Working in this team is like . . . (insert a simile) . . . because . . . (insert the reason).' You may need to clarify with the team what a simile actually is and give one or two hypothetical examples, such as 'Working in this team is like being on a roller coaster ride because it's so full of ups and downs'. This part of the exercise should take about ten or fifteen minutes.

Step 3: Write up the similes and the reason offered for them on a flip chart as in the fictional example below:

Working in this team is like . . .	Because . . .
Being on a roller-coaster	It's full of ups and downs
Playing for 'Rovers' (or other medium successful sports team)	We win some and we lose some
Being on stage every night	We are under so much scrutiny
Walking through the jungle	It's tough going and hard to know where we are headed
Being at a party at a house where you don't know many people	We don't know each other well as people but the atmosphere is slowly getting better

Step 4: Ask the team to review all the similes and assess what they say about the strengths and weaknesses of the team as it stands. Ask them which aspects they would like to *keep* and which aspects they need to *change*.

Step 5: Ask the team to repeat the simile process in trios but in this round vary the formula to describe what they would *like* working in the team to be like, as in the fictional example below:

We would like working in this team to be like . . .	Because . . .
Climbing Everest	There are big ups and there is a big achievement involved
Playing for 'Rangers' (or other highly successful sports team)	They work hard for each other and share great success – they win
Getting a standing ovation	We have our success acknowledged widely throughout the organisation and outside it
Walking across an open desert towards an oasis	It may be a long, tough walk but at least we can see where we are headed and it's worth getting there
Being at a party where all your best friends are there	It would be great to go to work and feel you are always working with people who know and like each other

Step 6: Ask the team to review the second set of similes and to discuss the key differences between the first and second sets.

Step 7: Ask the team to describe what they will need to change in specific terms if they are to have a team more like the second set of similes than the first – be aware there will usually be some things about the way the team currently sees itself that they would like to retain. Ask them too what they have learned about the nature of their team from the exercise.

Teams that organisational culture forgot

Interestingly, the most powerful examples of strong cultural influence I have encountered have been struggling teams whose primary purpose has been to affect *change* in the surrounding organisational culture. In a way it is as if by creating a 'change team' the organisations had infected themselves with a cultural virus (the 'change team' itself) and then created antibodies to maintain the status quo, immunising themselves against the very change they had committed to making. These change teams operated within a context in which both subtle and overt cultural factors acted against them in powerful ways to inhibit their effectiveness. They seemed to be fighting a battle their organisation would not let them win.

We will look now at striking examples of teams whose primary problems stemmed not so much from how they tried to work together as people but how they were being inhibited from becoming fully effective by the very context in which they were operating – the surrounding cultural context.

Case study one: the media change team

This team was formulated to help drive through a major culture change in a UK media organisation. The organisation itself held a high public profile and was frequently the subject of political debate and of media comment and speculation. The team was formed of executives from disparate parts of the organisation, and led by a highly respected senior manager who had a long and distinguished track record in the sector. The team comprised managers from various widespread departments and locations, with a broad spread of technical and professional skills. No one except the leader of this team was a full-time member, each of the others having at least some other responsibilities elsewhere. My role as team coach was to quickly get them to operate at full potential.

The first phases of the work with the team were unremarkable, consisting of a couple of team-building sessions to get to know each other, explore values and motivation, look at avenues for mutual support and make sure the team's initial working processes and protocols were effective. During this 'forming' phase the atmosphere was generally civil and professional but a little tense. A couple of the more macho characters locked horns lightly but overall the team gave an impression of confidence and capability.

However, as the project continued, frustrations with a perceived lack of progress began to creep in, and this frustration started to create a spikier atmosphere in the team sessions. The two most macho males had at least one quite scratchy spat, and one of them openly confronted the leader, frankly asserting that he was going to do what he was going to do and if she did not like it he would leave. The leader dealt with this particular protest extremely skilfully, refusing to be drawn into a stand-off.

The team was full of very strong personalities and there were numerous interpersonal tensions. But they were broadly able to deal with these by open discussion, feedback sessions, and sheer professional common sense. But as this 'storming' phase turned gradually into 'norming' and 'performing' a number of other, external pressures began to become more apparent.

Firstly, the team did not seem really clear as to its role as change agents: were they supposed to be facilitating change by coaching, mentoring and advising within the organisation or were they were supposed to be coercing and enforcing? What was their real mandate? And who decided the mandate?

Secondly, it became apparent that at least some of the team members were personally and politically attached to their own parts of the organisation and were engaged in furthering the interest of those parts even at the expense of the pan-corporate aims they were supposed to be working towards collectively.

Thirdly, it eventually became clear that all the team's proposed actions were overtly or subtly tested to ensure that everything the team did would meet with the approval of the organisation's chief executive, a man known to insist on things going his way. His presence was like a shadow over the team and for a long time a powerful 'elephant in the room' – something everyone knew was there but no one referred to.

Fourthly, it emerged that the team as a whole did not really grasp the full extent of the work they were engaged in. It was a massive project, but for several sessions no one admitted that they were unsure what was really going on – and was supposed to be going on – across the whole project. As individuals they were also unsure as to where their contributions were supposed to fit in.

It was by no means a neat and tidy process but gradually they grew to recognise these major issues and began to address them. Issue one, that of the *role* of the team, took a lot of bottoming out. They had long discussions about the organisation's values and the values of the team members themselves. The majority conviction of the team was that they should act as coaches, mentors and advisers rather than as enforcers. But there were also voices in the team which argued that as the changes *had* to happen it was disingenuous of the team to pretend that they were only facilitating – surely they had to be clear about the changes and insist upon them. The counter argument was that as the changes were primarily about promoting staff involvement and empowerment across the organisation it would be ideologically paradoxical to impose the means by which this was done – comparable, as one of the group said, to President Bush Senior's pronouncement that he would 'make the world democratic'.

Issue two – that of individuals acting in the interest of their own parts of the organisation - was even tougher. It was a sensitive topic to broach in any direct way, not least because it was difficult to prove. As coach, I became aware of the issue from corridor conversations and from occasional cryptic comments from within the group. Eventually there was a small number of open challenges about the behaviour of individuals, and this gave me the opportunity to make the tensions explicit and to gain formal commitment to what they expected of each other.

The third issue was particularly sensitive because it was hard for the team, and for the leader in particular, to recognise the pervasive influence of the organisation's chief executive. It fell to me to point out the regularity with which the team would say something like 'Well we can't do this because [the CEO] wouldn't like it'. This was the major cultural issue inhibiting the team – the fact that in this particular organisation no matter what pronouncements about consultation and staff involvement were made, what the boss wanted was still what really counted. It was to prove of absolutely critical importance that the team had been originally set up with the enthusiastic backing of the previous CEO. At first it was not really clear how much of his agenda was shared by the new CEO. This became the subject of intense team discussion. Could they follow their brief and their convictions and risk the disapproval of the new big chief? This issue was one of particular concern for the team leader, who bore overall responsibility for the actions of her team and who had to explain personally to the CEO what the team was doing and why.

A clear positive to come out of this difficult issue in terms of the internal dynamic of the team was the building of a committed resolve to stand by the team leader, to 'speak with one tongue' outside the team and to take the risk together of doing what they thought was right. However, this was not a blank cheque – the issue of the CEO's influence and presence never went away and was one the team ruminated over repeatedly. At one point I commented that it felt as if the CEO was 'always with us in the room', and the team agreed. There is no doubt that the team felt that ultimately they would have to toe the line; in other words, they had to go along with the CEO at least in appearances and for many of the big issues. But as a politically astute group they were also able to find subtle ways around things that were difficult for him to spot.

The fourth issue – that of everyone needing a clear understanding of the scope and remit of the whole project – was dealt with by conducting a monumental mapping exercise. I created a huge wall chart out of flip paper and masking tape and spent a day downloading information and building a systematic picture of the project in terms of criteria such as location, importance, interdependencies, responsibilities, political sensitivities and numerous technical and financial considerations. The team photographed it in detail so that each member would have a clear record and could refer back to it. One pleasing side-effect of this exercise was the reassurance and confidence it seemed to give the team: everyone had more or less assumed they personally were the only ones who did not know what was what. To have a picture of the project in all its complexity, and to realise they had all been in the same boat in not understanding it had a markedly reassuring effect.

It would be good to be able to report that this team coaching assignment had a clear, neat happy ending but few such team assignments are like that. In essence the project and the team began to lose momentum. Individuals from the team were drawn back to their day jobs and new members came and went with a frequency that made it hard to maintain coherence and impetus. The team leader herself became distracted by other issues and ultimately the team's work lost its sense of priority in an organisation where the agenda moved on according to wider political concerns – in essence the CEO's priorities moved on, and this had a direct impact on the team. Team meetings became less frequent and I was called in less often until the project effectively withered on the vine of corporate indifference.

What I tried to do

The main focus in working with this team had been on the team itself and how they worked together – as had been contracted. This was a striking example of how difficult it could be to even name, let alone deal effectively with, deep-rooted organisational cultural factors that exerted an irresistible force on the behaviour and the thinking of the team.

What could I have done differently? What would you have done? There remains a nagging anxiety that somehow I could have helped the team to stand up for itself more strongly. But the reality was almost certainly that the team could not afford to risk this – their very existence hung by a thread consisting essentially of the opinion of the CEO. Like most teams within the organisation they existed by playing the politics as best as they could.

Case study two: the emergency services change team

This team was, like the media team, selected from various parts of the organisation to affect corporate change, in this case a radical programme of change centred on core management and working practices. The organisation itself is charged with the provision of vital emergency services to a large urban population. The preoccupation of the organisation was response times – getting to emergencies on time and dealing with them quickly. This pressure on response times was generated by central government edict and was frequently the subject of comment and criticism by the national media.

The job of the team was to support and drive through changes to working practice that signalled a real shift of cultural emphasis, moving from a direct command-and-control ethos (this was a uniformed organisation) to one of greater staff involvement. My role was to support the team in its formative stages and coach it to perform to its potential.

I conducted a preliminary set of interviews with the team members. One outcome of this was to reveal a somewhat unorthodox leadership structure, with leadership being shared part-time between a senior organisational development (OD) manager and a senior operations manager. Both had onerous and diverse responsibilities within their own departments and the operations manager in particular felt her primary obligations were to operational matters rather than to the change team.

At the team's first meeting the interpersonal dynamics of the day felt reasonably positive, with a friendly and mutually supportive tone. They were able to move through the agenda, which aimed to put in place some fundamentals about how they saw their role and how they planned to work together, with what seemed like ease.

Against this, final membership of the team had not yet been finalised, leading to a feeling that they would have to begin developing the team all over again once the full team was assembled. There was also a nagging feeling from some parts of the team that this project was somehow something of a side show in organisational terms. There was also a distinct feeling that the shared leadership was in itself producing undercurrents of competitiveness, not just between the leaders but between the various parts of the team that saw their primary loyalty as falling with one leader or the other.

For me, additional frustration came with the difficulty of arranging subsequent team sessions. Sometimes these were arranged but were cancelled as operational issues got in the way. The operations manager in particular seemed difficult to pin down, and I began to wonder if it might become necessary to question her commitment. The second session involved a substantially different cast with two brand new members and one of the original members gone – a big shift in a team of only seven. The need to address hard business issues seemed to put pressure on time that should have been devoted to looking at how the team was working.

Subsequent private conversations with individual team members have revealed a general sense of disappointment with the project, particularly with the level and quality of its leadership, despite the continuation of at least superficially cordial relationships. What has also emerged is a frustration with the wider organisation. Numerous anecdotes seemed to support the growing theory that, whereas the organisational hierarchy would 'talk the talk' when it came to backing the cultural changes the team was charged with promoting, when it came to a tension between backing the changes and meeting any operational pressures, the fixation with response times and the 'old' style of leadership would be pursued without blinking.

Perhaps the most telling anecdote concerned a recent leadership conference in the organisation. One of the change team's leaders made a passionate and compelling speech calling on all senior leaders to support the changes and the work of the team: whilst he was talking, a team member present at the conference noticed that many of the delegates took the opportunity to check their blackberries and generally 'switch off' as if sensing that this speech did not really matter to them.

At time of writing there exists something of a crisis of confidence within this team, and even individual relationships have become strained. This strain has developed in a context in which individual behaviour, competence, personality and values should really have produced an effective team with a pleasant and supportive working climate. But like the media team, they operated in a cultural context where they were only allowed to challenge so much, and therefore to survive they were obliged to tolerate the cultural shackles within which they operate.

What I tried to do

In addition to the more general processes of team coaching – initial interviews, report writing, construction of an agenda to look at launching the team effectively, goal setting, looking at working protocols, relationship building and so forth – I attempted to make the team more aware of the influence of the surrounding culture. I explored ways in which the team could act more cohesively in presenting a united front to the wider organisation, and have a more effective upward influence, on a one-to-one basis, on members of the senior management team.

Summary

Interest in cultural aspects of organisational life continues to develop. This is true both in the academic sphere and in the world of practitioners who aim to provide practical maps, tools and skills for helping to navigate cultural and inter-cultural landscapes.

Most teams in the UK will be operating in a multi-cultural environment and are likely to be composed of team members from more than one national, social or cultural background. One interesting company, KnowledgeWorks Ltd, promises 'Inter-culturally intelligent consulting', and amongst other things offers fascinating tools and metrics that allow individuals and teams to develop sophisticated awareness of their cultural influences. Some understanding of culture is a must for the team coach and team leader. This awareness combined with lessons drawn from systems thinking offers a set of transformational possibilities and viewpoints that adds a whole different perspective to more traditional concepts of team dynamics.

Key learning points

- All teams are subject to influences from their surrounding organisational culture – they are not separate systems of their own to be understood purely in terms of their internal dynamics.
- Organisational culture can be understood at both superficial levels and also at the deeper levels of values, beliefs and identity.
- Internal culture-change teams can be particularly vulnerable to conscious and unconscious resistance from the 'owners' of the existing culture.
- Working with teams to help them become more aware of their cultural environment can help equip them to work more effectively within it.
- The language that teams use both reflects and creates the microculture in which they operate.

Reflective questions

If you are leading a team:

- What are the dominant metaphors for use in your team and what do they say about its strengths and weaknesses?
- What is the surrounding organisational culture and what is the influence of this culture on your team?
- How could you work more effectively within the surrounding culture?

If you are coaching a team:

- How can you take surrounding cultural influences into account in your work with the team?
- What are your own cultural assumptions about how a team 'should' operate?
- How are the systems and cultural influences within which your team operates impacting upon behaviour?

8   Further resources for team leaders and coaches

The team coach needs an array of resources to bring to the process, above and beyond his or her group skills and background knowledge. This chapter points to a selection that I have used personally or have very close knowledge of and can vouch for in terms of their application. Where relevant, within each category of resources the chapter will cover:

- Uses and benefits
- Factors indicating appropriateness of use or otherwise
- Possible pitfalls

Executive coaching courses and training

There is a vast selection of providers to choose from and the marketplace is confusing and of widely divergent quality. If you are looking for training in executive or business coaching, you should consider the following questions:

- Does the company or organisation offer courses accredited by any of the major coaching bodies such as the EMCC, ICF or AC?
- Do they take time to talk with you about what is involved and about your individual needs?
- Do they over-promise, for example by claiming to turn you into a competent coach over a weekend?
- Do they offer professional qualifications?
- Can they provide referees for you to talk to about their courses?
- Do they offer a proprietary model that claims pre-eminence over all other models or do they offer best practice drawn from multiple sources? The latter approach is likely to be more rounded and grounded.
- Have they contributed to the development of the field through writing and publishing?

- Do they themselves practise as executive coaches as well as teach? This is a crucial test

It is hard for me to remain unbiased here given my close association with this organisation, but Management Futures Ltd fulfils all these requirements, offering:

- Executive coaching skills training
- Diplomas and certificates in coaching and mentoring – awarded by the Institute of Leadership and Management (ILM) at Level 7 and endorsed by the European Mentoring and Coaching Council (EMCC)
- Training in team coaching
- Leadership skills training
- One-to-one executive coaching

Management Futures Ltd
37 Grays Inn Road, London, WC1X 8PQ, UK
+44 (0)207 2424030
info@managementfutures.co.uk
www.managementfutures.co.uk

The Academy of Executive Coaching, another good source of training in team coaching with programmes accredited by EMCC, ICF, AC and Middlesex University, offers a wide range of coaching courses and qualifications, including a Masters degree in coaching.

The Academy of Executive Coaching
+44 (0)1727 864806
executivecoaching@aoec.com
www.aoec.com

Other providers worth considering include Ashridge Business School and the OCM.

Outdoor providers

A good outdoor provider can offer an inspirational setting and create a programme that can help a team to develop confidence, cohesion and learning as well as tap into previously unrecognised talents and strengths. Part of my own background has been working on team development in the outdoors, and there is no doubt that when an outdoor-based course goes well it can have a power and intensity in accelerating and enriching team development that is hard to beat.

The roots of outdoor-based team development training in the UK stem most directly from the Outward Bound Trust model, in which learning and development was largely thought to be achieved directly from the power of working together, sometimes in adversity, in challenging outdoor environments. Originally this kind of development model was aimed primarily at young people as part of the core ethos of the Outward Bound charitable trust. Another leading player in this sector, the Brathay Hall Trust, was established with a similar charitable purpose – to aid the development of young people. Both these centres were established shortly after the Second World War and have gone on in recent decades to develop specific courses and products aimed at managers and leaders from the business and organisational world. They employ trainers with business experience and facilitation/coaching skills who work alongside technically qualified outdoor experts. Amongst other centres with good reputations is Impact International, which in addition to offering outdoor-based learning experiences offers programmes based on community involvement and sustainability projects.

Each of these organisations is based in the English Lake District but all work virtually anywhere in the UK and will work abroad too – especially Impact, which has numerous global branches.

The old-fashioned notion that such courses are all to do with 'character building' and involve significant hardship and 'roughing it' is still around in places. But the reality is that modern outdoor team development training is provided for the most part by sophisticated organisations fully in touch with the realities of modern organisational life. Many trainers will be qualified in a number of fields including psychology, the application of psychometric tools, Neuro-Linguistic programming and coaching.

The central ethos of such centres is 'learning by doing'. They provide a structured sequence of experiences including problem-solving exercises, complex projects and outdoor-based tasks including expeditions. The 'doing' part is supported by extensive facilitated reviews aimed at drawing individual and team learning from the experiences. This 'do and review' model is supported by appropriate theory and by sessions dedicated to the application of learning back in the work place. This learning model broadly follows the familiar Kolb learning cycle (Kolb and Fry, 1975) and therefore has most individual learning styles covered.

A good outdoor centre offering team development should:

- Have impeccable health and safety credentials
- Offer complete respect and consideration to participants – for example never offering nasty 'surprise' activities or springing tricks of the 'what you didn't know . . .' variety during problem-solving exercises
- Be able to offer course experiences suitable for people who have disabilities

- Offer training staff with real business/organisational experience as well as relevant academic/professional qualifications – both male and female
- Offer a wide range of learning experiences enabling all kinds of people to learn – not just 'outdoorsy' types
- Be sophisticated in understanding and responding to cultural issues
- Offer a relatively high trainer – participant ratio for most types of programme – one trainer to eight participants is about right
- Offer flexibility of course design aimed at the development needs of a particular team, not just an off-the-shelf experience
- Involve participants in the development of their course, offering choices to them as their experience proceeds
- Never, ever apply macho pressure to participants to undertake activities they do not want to do – whilst offering respectful encouragement and coaching support to attempt a degree of 'stretch' where appropriate
- Provide comfortable accommodation, essential outdoor kit and good food

Team development experiences can be structured in short bites of as little as one day, although I firmly believe that the most powerful experiences are built over three days or more. They are especially valuable when:

- A team wants to integrate new members quickly
- A team has big challenges to face
- A team wants a 'stretch' experience
- A team wants to look for untapped resources

Contact details for outdoor providers

Impact International
Cragwood House, Windermere, Cumbria, LA23 1LQ, UK
+44 (0)1539 488333
www.impactinternational.com

Brathay Trust
Brathay Hall, Ambleside, Cumbria, LA22OHP, UK
brathay@brathay.org.uk
www.brathay.org.uk

Outward Bound Professional
Gate House, Eskdale Green, Holmrook, Cumbria, CA19 1TE, UK
+44 (0) 8702 423028
training@obprofessional.co.uk
www.obprofessional.co.uk

Other useful organisations

The Tavistock Institute
30 Tabernacle Street, London, EC2A 4UE, UK
+44 (0)207 4170407
hello@tavinstitute.org

This is a not-for-profit organisation that has a strong track record and reputation for researching and applying social science knowledge to contemporary issues and problems. They engage in a wide variety of individual and group interventions across a wider range of constituencies and are renowned for their research. They have a particular commitment to working with and understanding the unconscious processes that underpin much problematic behaviour. They have many publications and courses and would be a great place to contact if you wished to deepen your understanding of psychodynamic processes and theories.

RSVP Design Ltd
2 Darluith Park, Brookfield, Johnstone, PA5 8OD, UK
+44 (0)1505 382422
www.rsvpdesign.co.uk

RSVP Design Ltd manufactures and markets a wide variety of experiential exercises aimed at developing teams and with other management development applications. I have had personal experience of using a number of their products and can vouch for their quality, simplicity of use and face validity. Their website describes their product range and there is a link to a YouTube website that allows you to see some of their games and simulations in use. The prices of their products range from around £20 to several thousand pounds, with most of their range priced in the hundreds of pounds.

OPP
Elsfield Hall, 15-17 Elsfield Way, Oxford, OX2 8EP, UK
+44 (0)845 603 9958
enquiry@opp.eu.com
www.opp.eu.com

In the UK the prominent supplier of psychometric instruments, including training in their use and qualification is OPP. They also operate in twenty-five other countries including many European countries and the USA. They offer a wide range of instruments and training including MBTI Step 1, MBTI Step 2, 16PF, FIRO-B and Strong Interest Inventory. Their qualifications are endorsed by the British Psychological Society (BPS).

Mind Management
PO Box 1, Battle, East Sussex, TN33 OHY, UK
+44 (0)1424 775100
thinking@hbdi.co.uk

and

Herrmann International
794 Buffalo Creek Road, Lake Lure, NC 28746, USA
+1 828 625 9153
service@hbdi.com
www.hbdi.com

Another interesting questionnaire is the Herrmann Brain Dominance Instrument or HBDI. This was developed by Ned Herrmann in the United States in the 1970s and 1980s. The instrument measure brain functioning and at the simplest level explores how we use our brains, in particular investigating the ways in which we favour either the left brain or right brain. Herrmann was particularly interested in the application of this knowledge to allow us to use more creativity. The instrument is simple to interpret and is especially useful for team development, providing a great deal of insight into how our thinking patterns create much of our behaviour. Teams using it benefit from insight into how they communicate together, how thinking styles impact team culture and from learning how to be more creative.

This has a different feel from a 'regular' psychometric and although the company that offers it in the UK – Mind Management – says it is validated in the USA it is unclear as to who has done this validation. Herrmann International is the main body organising certification and licensing. My recommendation would be to read *The Creative Brain* by Ned Herrmann (1989) to get a feel for the instrument.

Training in facilitation

The Chartered Institute of Personnel and Development (CIPD) run basic and advanced open courses in facilitation skills. They can be found at:

CIPD
151 The Broadway, London, SW19 1JQ, UK
+44 (0)208 6126200
www.cipd.co.uk

Reputable courses in facilitation are also offered by The Roffey Park Institute:

Roffey Park Institute
Forest Road, Horsham, West Sussex, RH12 4TB, UK
+44 (0)1293 851644
info@roffeypark.com
www.roffeypark.com

Games and Simulations

There are plenty of manuals and resource books that offer management team games and simulations. Full-blown business simulations tend to be complex exercises that hypothesise specific business scenarios such as starting up a new business. If you Google 'business simulations' you will be met with a bewildering array of sources, organisations and websites. One I have found useful and practical is www.plymouth.ac.uk which takes quite a serious approach to pointing you towards resources for what they call SGRPs – Simulations, Games and Role Plays. They have a directory of resources including relevant societies and associations, publications, journals, resources in higher education and a selection of 'approved' SGRPs.

The key for the team coach is to find a selection of exercises that produce consistently predictable and powerful learning. You need to understand a game thoroughly, including the various ways it can turn out in terms of how teams might behave. You also need to have flexible means of reviewing it: it is one thing to review an exercise in which a team has triumphed and quite another to review the same exercise if the team has messed it up. I include below a selection of portable, easy-to-use games that have stood me in good stead for many years.

'Red/Blue' – an exercise to examine trust in teams

I learned this exercise over twenty years ago and have used it scores of times since with good results over a wide range of groups. You can find various versions of it, and it is sometimes called The Prisoner's Dilemma. I have yet to find a formula to beat the one I describe here. The overall point of the exercise is to explore dynamics of trust between team members or between one team and another, and to learn how certain types of communication behaviour can strongly influence the development and maintenance of trust – positively or negatively. The degree to which team members trust each other is an extremely important aspect of team functioning. I have yet to see a team function at full potential if trust is low. Low trust inhibits communication and weakens mutual support, creating a climate of fear and defensiveness in which individuals rarely if ever put forward their best effort.

The rules, set up and scoring system can appear complex at first glance, so do take time to understand them. In essence each group has ten opportunities to signal either cooperation or competitive intent – red is a cooperative play and blue a competitive one. If both teams play red throughout it can end up as quite a tame exercise – although one which can usefully confirm and highlight the essentially cooperative nature of the team. When there is some blue thrown in it can become highly competitive and even lead to mutual failure – the lose-lose scenario.

Running Red/Blue

- Separate the group into two by arbitrary means – perhaps just by asking one half of the group to go to another room.
- Consider asking one person per sub-group to act as observer for the exercise. If you take this option, ask the observers to sit quietly away from the group without interacting, and to record verbatim comments from their group as the exercise proceeds through the rounds.
- Visit each group in turn and give them the instruction sheet below. Explain to them that both groups have the same sheet of instructions to work from. Also explain that in your role as 'The Trainer' you will only be visiting to record their round-by-round decisions and will not otherwise engage with them.
- Give each group a few minutes to understand the instructions on the sheet and then visit them in turn to check their understanding.
- Make it clear that it is against the rules to attempt to communicate with the other team by any means other than those stipulated by the exercise instructions – for example, no use of mobile phones is allowed.
- When both groups are clear about the process, tell them the game will begin at once, and let them know they will need to decide their choice of play quite quickly between rounds – the game should take no longer than twenty to thirty minutes to run.
- Ask Group One to declare a colour – red or blue. Ask them to record their decision, and also keep a record yourself.
- Ask Group Two to do the same.
- After both groups have declared their play, tell each group what the other has played – this will enable both groups to know the current score.
- Repeat the process for rounds two, three and four.
- After round four, ask each group in turn if they wish to confer with the other group – do not tell either group what the other has decided until both groups have declared.
- If both groups agree, have a representative from each group meet each other on neutral ground, and give them up to five minutes to have an open discussion on how they wish to conduct the rest of the exercise

- If one or both groups decide not to confer, simply carry on as before, asking the groups to choose colours on a round-by-round basis.
- Repeat the scoring as before for rounds four to eight.
- After round eight, repeat the invitation to confer as in round four, using the same procedures.
- Continue the rounds until round ten, and then invite both groups to reassemble together for a review.

Red/Blue instruction sheet

Task:

To end up with a positive score for your group.

Procedure:

The Trainer will visit your group and ask you to decide whether to play RED or to play BLUE. The Trainer will not tell you which colour the other group has played.

When both groups have declared their play, the Trainer will announce the colours which have been played.

Play will be scored as follows:

If Group 1 plays	and Group 2 plays	The score is: Group1	Group 2
Red	Red	+ 3	+ 3
Red	Blue	– 6	+ 6
Blue	Red	+ 6	– 6
Blue	Blue	– 3	– 3

There will be ten rounds.

After the fourth round the Trainer will ask the groups whether they wish to have a conference. This conference will only take place at the request of both groups. If either does not wish to confer then no meeting will take place.

After the eighth round there will be a second opportunity for a conference should both groups wish it.

The ninth and tenth round score double.

Reviewing Red/Blue

- Bring both groups back together. Be aware that if either group has 'shafted' the other then feelings can run quite high – even if there is a lot of laughter and joking. If this is the case, it is best usually to allow the teams to let off a bit of steam before attempting a formal review.

- Ask each group in turn to describe both their thinking and their feelings as they went through the exercise. If you have used observers you can ask them to add their observations at this stage – verbatim quotations are often both interesting and amusing. Whilst each group is giving its account ask the other group to be quiet and listen.
- When both groups have given their account there is usually the need to allow a little more free discussion before continuing the review – groups are often keen to question each other about their motivations for particular decisions, particularly if there has been a win–lose or a lose – lose outcome.

Depending on the conduct of the exercise the following are the review points that arise most frequently. Each of them can be discussed both as theoretical points and as a way of exploring trust and communication issues within the team.

1   Early communications – first impressions – are extremely powerful. When one or both groups opt to play blue early it is hard for them to build trust subsequently.
2   Face-to-face communications virtually always carry more weight than indirect ones such as email or even phone. When teams agree to co-operate during a face-to-face negotiation – particularly when they shake hands on their commitment – there is rarely a breach of trust afterwards. It does happen occasionally that teams confer face to face, agree to cooperate, and then one or both teams breaks their word, but this is quite rare and usually provokes outrage.
3   The exercise shows how easy it can be to set up competitive dynamics – simply creating two groups and placing them in two different rooms is usually enough to set up a strong 'them and us' feeling, regardless of previous relationships. Are there any 'structural' factors which might be setting up uncooperative or competitive attitudes within the team?
4   Competitive instincts – when are they useful and when destructive? When one or other group has played competitively they often assert that competitiveness is both necessary and fun in team and organisational life. This can be the trigger for a productive discussion on the nature and value of competitive behaviour. For example if competitive behaviours and attitudes exist between team members this seems more obviously destructive, but if competition is directed at external competitors this can be seen as productive.

Blindfold Square and Double Blindfold Square

These two simple exercises are excellent ways of looking at team communication issues, particularly those of listening and planning. You will need to check with your team that they are happy to work on something active and mildly physical, and be ready to offer an observer role for any team members who are not keen to take part. Occasionally someone will feel uncomfortable at the idea of wearing a blindfold. Four is the smallest number that can participate in this version, and eight is probably ideal, although up to around twelve is acceptable – especially if someone wants to take an observer role. The simplest version runs as follows.

Blindfold Square

You will need a rope and some space – probably outdoors – for this exercise. The very best kind of rope is old climbing rope – about 15 metres is ideal. Any fairly thick, soft, non-abrasive rope will do though – a hardware store can supply this. You will also need a blindfold for each participant. At a pinch those sold in chemists and travel shops as eye rests will do though I had some made up using thicker material that ensures a complete black-out so that participants are not tempted to peek.

Lay the rope out on the floor in an 'S' or 'U' shape, ensuring there are no snags or tangles. Ask all participants to put on their blindfolds and help them to do so if necessary. Ask them to listen carefully to the following spoken instructions:

- The aim of the exercise is for the group to construct a *perfect square*, at approximately waist height above the ground, using the whole of the rope.
- By the end of the exercise the members of the team should be distributed as evenly as possible at the corners of the square, supporting the rope (for example, if there are 8 members there would be 2 at each corner, if only 7 members one corner would have only 1 person).
- The only way to communicate during the exercise is verbally or by touch – blindfolds must stay on at all times.
- There is no strict time limit but the team should aim for about twenty minutes maximum to complete the exercise.

Check that everyone has understood the instructions and mention the following safety constraints: team members should move slowly and avoid sudden or erratic movements. Explain also that you will ensure no one bumps into anything or walks towards anything dangerous.

When these instructions have been given and questions answered, hand one end of the rope at random to a member of the group and let them begin.

When observing the group in action it is useful to watch out for the following:

- Who speaks and who stays quiet?
- What is the level of listening like?
- Does the group spend time planning or simply launch into action?
- How involved is everyone in the group?
- What behaviours appear to be helping or hindering?
- How is the standard 'perfect' (remember you asked for a *perfect* square) judged and who has input into setting standards within the group?
- How does the group handle different ideas and viewpoints – even conflict?
- Who appears to lead? How effective is their leadership?

Reviewing Blindfold Square

As with any task-based problem-solving exercise there is a core of questions, based on the above observation points, that are useful to have at your disposal, including:

- What went well?
- What went less well?
- What might we do differently next time given a similar task?
- How does how we worked together relate to how we approach working in the real world?
- What did individuals contribute?
- How did we approach planning?
- What leadership was there – and who provided it?

With this particular exercise I think there are some particular aspects that require specific questions. For example:

- How well did we listen to each other?
- How fully were people included?
- How far did we check that everyone understood the process?
- How did individuals *feel*? (A particularly useful question if some people, as frequently happens, simply get left holding a rope for twenty minutes whilst louder people take over the exercise.)
- How did we approach standard-setting (who decides the square is perfect? And how is it decided?).

Blindfold Double Square

This exercise is a variant that is particularly useful for larger teams, and for teams where members do not necessarily work closely together for much of the time, or tend to work in sub-groups. It can also be extremely useful as an exercise when two or more teams are coming together to work for the first time, perhaps on a project or as part of cross-organisational working.

The absolute minimum number required for the exercise is seven. In this version the overall team is split into two groups, each with its own rope. The groups are separated by a short distance, and each group in turn is briefed separately. The instructions for each group are identical to those in the original blindfold square exercise, except that in addition to having to form the perfect square as before, they are told their square needs to intersect with the other group's square, to form a double-diamond of intersecting squares.

Reviewing Blindfold Double Square

The key to success for this version of the exercise is that the two teams recognise early on that collaboration between them is necessary. Groups vary wildly in terms of success in this exercise. It is important for the teams to consult each other early in the process about how to create the point of intersection. Sometimes one team calls across to another and is ignored. At other times both teams just concentrate on their own square and only when one is finished will they seek to make contact with the other team. I have seen on more than one occasion one team finish their square relatively quickly and then simply jeer at the other team as they struggle to complete theirs.

The key review points in this version are:

- How much is collaboration rather than competition assumed?
- How much is the exercise thought through as a joint effort?
- How did they manage communication between the teams?
- What analogies have they seen in the way they operate in real life?

The Ball Circle

This is an excellent multi-purpose exercise requiring nothing more than a small bag of soft juggling balls and a reasonable space, either indoors or outdoors. It can be used as:

- An ice-breaker
- An energiser
- An exercise to look at team communication
- An exercise to look at raising performance and ambition

Ask the team to form a circle. If you are indoors clear away any glasses or cups or anything else fragile that could be knocked over. Explain that the exercise has two phases.

The first phase is for the team to create a pattern with a single juggling ball. The pattern is created by throwing the ball *gently* to each other to create a pattern in which everyone receives the ball once before it goes back to the first thrower (you, the team coach). The only constraint is that no one can throw the ball to the person either side of them. This part of the task usually takes two or three goes before a pattern is established.

The second phase is about seeing how many balls the team can handle, using the same pattern. The team continues to throw the ball around the circle in the patterned sequence created in phase one. At intervals, feed in more balls. The idea is for the team to cope with as many balls in the air at once as possible. For health and safety reasons, if things get too hectic remind the team that they should throw gently even if they are in a hurry – even a soft juggling ball can carry a bit of impact if thrown too hard.

Teams vary a lot in how they respond to this exercise and in terms of performance. It is possible for a team to keep as many balls in the air as there are team members – although this rarely happens until they have practised several times. What generally happens over about twenty minutes is that the team moves from chaos and near panic to a rhythmic cohesion. This is more likely to happen if you get them to pause from time to time to review how they are handling the task. One useful mid-exercise review technique is to get them to have conversations with the people in the circle they are actually throwing to and receiving from, about how they are working together – things like eye-contact, signalling readiness, calling out names before throwing, and so on, are all useful means of improving performance.

Reviewing the Ball Circle

This apparently simple exercise can produce a surprisingly rich review and there are frequent 'ah-ha!' moments. Basic questions you can ask include:

- What analogies do you see with how the team works on the ball exercise and how it works in reality?
- What is it that makes the exercise *seem* difficult? Teams usually realise it is the *perception* of chaos and complexity that makes the exercise seem challenging.
- Individually, what do you need to focus on to make this exercise work? In fact individuals only need to really focus on the person they are throwing to and the person they are receiving from – this is a useful analogy for the need to keep centred and focused only on the parts of a team task or process that you are actually personally able to deal with, rather than being distracted by the chaos or 'interference' that can surround your work.
- How is a performance standard set? Who decides what the target should be? Who decides if the team is performing well, and against

what criteria? Are standards or goals understood and communicated to the whole team?
- How does the team deal with failure and mistakes? As opportunities to learn or as opportunities to blame?

With experience, you can tweak the exercise in various ways to adapt to different learning needs. In my experience some teams can get quite absorbed in this exercise and its analogies to both team and personal performance. It is also an exercise you can use from one session to another – some teams really look forward to seeing how well they can do and get quite addicted to the task.

Occasionally someone in the team will say they absolutely 'can't' catch. I have rarely found this to be absolutely true and in fact a lot of people surprise themselves with how well they can catch in the context of a supportive team environment. Clearly if they do not *want* to take part it is proper to respect this – I usually ask the person who wants to sit out the exercise to take an observer role and feed back their observations during the review process.

The Rope Trick

This is a wonderful little exercise to keep up your sleeve if you want to examine issues of ambition, belief, and assumptions of capability within a team. Some teams under-perform primarily because they have self-limiting assumptions about their performance capabilities and this simple exercise provides a means of examining attitudes in this important area.

You will need two metres (plus a few centimetres more to make the knot) of soft rope knotted to make a loop of two metres in circumference. Explain that the task is for the group to take five minutes to discuss how quickly they feel they could pass the whole group through the loop – including the opportunity to practise techniques. After five minutes ask them to say what they think their best time would be. Most teams will say something like a minute, perhaps thirty seconds. Then ask them to attempt to reach their target – allow them as many attempts as they want, within reason. After the team has attempted to reach their target, and even if they have succeeded, tell them that a high-performing team could achieve the task in no more than one second per person – for example, eight seconds for an eight-person team. Ask them if they would then like another go! Most teams are initially a little shocked that this is a reachable target, but do indeed have another go, raise their sights and successfully reach the more ambitious target. The trick is for two people to hold the rope, pass it quickly over everyone else in the team and then pass it over each other. Most teams can achieve this after two or three attempts.

Reviewing the Rope Trick

This exercise can lead to a discussion about ambition, challenge, goals and standards. Questions to ask might include:

- What might be limiting your ambition?
- What would it be like to perform at a higher level?
- What would have to change for you to raise your sights?
- What will you do in practice to raise performance expectations?

Sometimes a team will set the high-performance target immediately and achieve it. You can congratulate them on their achievement and engage them in a conversation about areas of their performance that are not at the same high standard.

Toy Production

This simple exercise is an excellent way of introducing discussion about creativity in teams. The fact is that management teams are increasingly asked to deal with situations where they have to manage more with fewer resources, or have to find new ways of working to tackle new operating conditions, such as changes in the market or new government requirements. It is rarely an option for a team to be able to sit back and carry on with 'business as usual'.

Some teams or individuals can be uncomfortable with the concept of creativity, worrying that it is something for 'artistic' types and somehow does not merit a real role in a serious workplace. This exercise offers an opportunity for teams to discuss how they can promote and support *practical* creativity in the cause of strategic planning, problem-solving or brainstorming.

Divide the team into two or three groups of at least three people – ideally with a separate room to work in for each team, but if not at least some working space somewhere away from each other. Give each team a copy of the following sheet of instructions.

Toy Production Challenge

At this time of year, the toy industry is working flat out to dream up and produce new exciting products for next Christmas. New ideas are at a premium, demands for high quality never fiercer, schedules have never been tighter or resources more stretched. In addition, there are new players in the market.

Your task is to work as a team to design and produce a new toy or game that could potentially see you take a market lead. You are in competition to produce a better product than your competitors, who have equal time and resources. A major buyer will be reviewing the products in thirty minutes. He will want to see you demonstrate your game or toy in such a way that your competitors are able to play it or use it within minutes, so you will have to be able to explain the game or toy to them effectively.

Your resources will be: a few sheets of coloured card, one string of paper clips, one roll of tape, rubber bands, coloured pens, index cards, two coloured hats, six balloons, two whistles, scissors, a highlighter pen. You are not allowed to use anything else you may have with you.

Running Toy Production

Please note that you can make up the list of available materials to suit what you have to hand or the particular opportunities or constraints your working environment may suggest. Once your sub-teams have the instructions and their allotted materials you can confine yourself to an observational role. After thirty minutes, stop the teams and ask them in turn to demonstrate the use of their game or toy, ideally by getting one of the other teams to try it out.

My experience is that teams often become really creative in this exercise and sometimes really clever toys or games are made. Following the action phase, a review can focus on the following key questions:

- What helped you in your creative process?
- What if anything hindered you?
- How can you bring your learning from this exercise into your creative thinking at work?

As an aside, I ran this exercise for several years as part of a two-day course called 'Imagineering' for the BBC's technical resource departments. The participants were almost all highly technical people such as engineers, technicians and resource managers but they invariably found the exercise absorbing and reported that it helped them to focus on how to build creative opportunities for their own teams. One consistent but perhaps surprising feature of the reviews we held was how much the principle of 'less is more' applies to creativity: when resources are limited and time is short, minds are concentrated on making the most of what there is and creativity can flourish.

Audits

There are various audits on team effectiveness available. Audits are a simple way for a team to assess their current effectiveness and to monitor how they are progressing. Here are a couple of simple and robust formats you can use or adapt for use with many teams:

Format one: How we work together

Criteria	Strongly agree 5	Agree 4	Undecided 3	Disagree 2	Strongly disagree 1
Cooperation: Team members work well together.					
Communication: Our ability to give and receive necessary information is one of our strengths.					
Goals: Goal setting is truly a team activity.					
Creativity: Innovation is encouraged and rewarded.					
Conflict: Disagreements are faced up to and worked through fully.					
Support: Praise and recognition are given enthusiastically.					
Mutual respect: Team members show appreciation to one another and avoid sarcasm, put downs etc.					
Commitment: Everyone is dedicated to furthering team goals.					
Atmosphere: The climate is such that people are willing to put forth their best effort.					
Cohesion: Team members see themselves as a tight-knit group.					
Pride: People feel good about being a team member.					
Decisions: Everyone has the fullest opportunity to participate in decisions that affect the group.					
Openness: Everyone is encouraged to say what is on his/her mind without fear of reprisal.					
Trust: Team members feel that no one in the group will take advantage of them in any way.					
Review: The team reviews its own functioning regularly on a frank and open basis.					
Belonging: I feel that I am treated as a full member of this team and feel very much part of it.					

Criteria	Strongly agree 5	Agree 4	Undecided 3	Disagree 2	Strongly disagree 1
Leadership: Our team leader is key to our effectiveness.					
Feedback to Leader: The boss is very open to suggestions about improvement to his/her performance.					

Format two: Effective teamwork audit

Thirty years of research has helped identify the factors associated with effective team work.

Score your team as it currently is in your view on these factors.
Scoring key: 1 = pretty dire; 2 = room for improvement; 3 = OK; 4 = very strong

Clarity about overall goals. The team knows where it is going, why, and what competitive challenges it faces to get there. It is well on its way to excellent performance. *1 2 3 4*

Clarity about individual roles. Team members are clear about their own and other individuals' roles. Their tasks are achievable, thanks to the way the work is organised. *1 2 3 4*

Recognition. The climate is one where a discriminating generosity prevails about other people's work. When people do good work, it is noticed and commented on immediately, with the most recognition going to the best performer. In this climate, it is not left to the team leader to give such acknowledgement – it is common practice for all team members. Equally, there is more emphasis on recognition than on criticism. People know how to ask for, give and receive feedback. *1 2 3 4*

Conflict is worked on: neither avoided nor deliberately fanned. Conflict is about working better, not about interpersonal issues. *1 2 3 4*

Participation permeates everything the team does, from setting overall goals for the whole team, to influencing each other's objectives and negotiating or reviewing personal objectives. *1 2 3 4*

Performance standards are set at a level which is high enough to be challenging and inspiring. People continually strive to do the best possible work without being constrained by fear of failure. Moreover, each person's performance, as well as the whole team's, is evaluated according to these standards. *1 2 3 4*

Relationships inside the team are based on mutual trust *1 2 3 4*
and friendliness: when one individual needs help, the others are
quick to respond. The manager supports team members when
he or she believes they are right and people take pride in their
membership of the team.

Communication with other teams ensures that the team's *1 2 3 4*
work is well integrated with that of other teams, with ideas,
thoughts and suggestions circulating freely.

Relationships with other teams are characterised by trust so *1 2 3 4*
that when conflicts arise they can be dealt with swiftly and effectively without the need for umpires from senior management.

A useful tool kit for the team coach

All the exercises above can be accomplished with a remarkably small – and
cheap – tool kit. It is useful to carry a small kit around with you as team coach
so that you can offer flexibility and be ready with alternatives to what you had
planned. My kit – which fits into a sports bag – comprises the following:

- A small bag of felt tip pens for meta-planning or other creative exercises (and because you cannot always be sure the venue you are using
  will have pens that work).
- A small bag of juggling balls – twelve is enough
- two fifteen-metre lengths of soft, non-abrasive rope such as climbing
  rope
- A bag of fifteen blindfolds, ideally of a good heavy quality (I had mine
  made at £5 each)
- one metre length of rope knotted into a loop
- Post-it® notes – largest size – for meta-planning or 'toy production'
- Blu-tack
- Masking tape – great for making wall screens out of bits of flip chart
- A few copies of the 'red/blue' instructions
- A small bag of bits and pieces – balloons, card, paperclips, scissors,
  pencils and so on for 'toy production'

References

Adair, J. (1973) *Action-Centred Leadership*, McGraw-Hill, London.

Bandler, R. (1985) *Using Your Brain – For a Change*, Real People Press, Boulder.

Belbin, R.M. (1981) *Management Teams: Why They Succeed or Fail*, Butterworth-Heinemann, Oxford.

Berne, E. (1975) *The Structure and Dynamics of Organisations and Groups*, Ballantine, New York.

Bion, W.R. (1968) *Experiences in Groups and Other Papers*, Tavistock Publications, London.

Branson, R. (2010) *Business Stripped Bare: Adventures of a Global Entrepreneur*, Virgin Books, New York.

Briggs Myers, I. (1995) *Gifts Differing: Understanding Personality Type*, Davis Black, Davis.

Clutterbuck, D. (2007) *Coaching the Team at Work*, Nicholas Brealey, London.

Covey, S. (2004) *The Seven Habits of Highly Effective People*, Simon & Schuster, New York.

Gallwey, W.T. (1986) *The Inner Game of Tennis*, Random House, New York.

Gallwey, W.T. (1997) *The Inner Game of Work*, Random House, New York.

Goleman, D. (1996) *Emotional Intelligence*, Bloomsbury, London.

Goleman, D. (1999) *Working with Emotional Intelligence*, Bloomsbury, London.

Hare, R.D. (1993) *Without Conscience: The Disturbing World of the Psychopaths Among Us*, Guilford Press, New York.

Herrmann, N. (1989) *The Creative Brain*, McGraw-Hill, London

Hofstede, G. and Hofstede, G.J. (2005) *Cultures and Organisations: Software of the Mind*, McGraw-Hill, London.

Honey, P. and Mumford, A. (1982) *The Manual of Learning Styles*, Peter Honey Publications, Maidenhead.

Honey, P. and Mumford, A. (1983) *Using Your Learning Styles*, Peter Honey Publications, Maidenhead.

Jung, C.G. (1991) *The Archetypes and the Collective Unconscious* (Collected Works, vol. 9), Routledge, London. Translated R.F.C. Hull.

Kolb, D.A. and Fry, R. (1975) *Towards an Applied Theory of Experiential Learning*, John Wiley, London.

Kouzes, J.M. and Posner, B.Z. (1993) *Credibility: How Leaders Gain it and Lose it, Why People Demand it*, Jossey-Bass, San Francisco.

Lewin, K. and Lippitt, R. (1938) 'An experiential approach to the study of autocracy and democracy', *Sociometry*, vol. 1, pp. 292–300.

Litwin, G.H. and Stringer, R.A. (1969) *Motivation and Organisational Climate*, Harvard University Press, Cambridge.

Luft, J. (1969) *Of Human Interaction*, National Press, Palo Alto.

McGregor, R. (2006) *The Human Side of Enterprise* (Annotated Edition), McGraw-Hill Professional, London.

McKenna, P. (2006) *Instant Confidence*, Bantam, New York.

Maslow, A. (1987) *Motivation and Personality*, Longman, London.

Mayo, E. (1933) *The Human Problems of an Industrial Civilisation*, Macmillan, New York.

Morgan, G. (2006) *Images of Organisation*, Sage, Thousand Oaks.

Perls, F. (1969) *Gestalt Therapy Verbatim*, Real People Press, Boulder.

Rackham, N. (1995) *Spin-Selling*, Gower, Farnham.

Rath, T. and Harter, J. (2010) *Wellbeing: The Five Essential Elements*, Gallup Press, New York.

Revans, R.W. (1983) *The Origin and Goals of Action Learning*, Chartwell-Bratt, Bromley.

Rogers, C. (1961) *On Becoming a Person: A Therapist's View of Psychotherapy*, Constable, London.

Rogers, J. (2008) *Coaching Skills: A Handbook*, 2nd Edition McGraw-Hill, London.

Rogers, J. (2007) *Sixteen Personality Types: At Work in Organisations*, Management Futures Ltd, London.

Schein, E. (1988) *Process Consultation*, Addison-Wesley Publishing Company, Boston.

Seligman, M. and Csikszentmihalyi, M. (2000) 'Positive psychology: an introduction', *American Psychologist*, 55(1), pp. 5–14.

Simon, G.K. (1996) *In Sheep's Clothing*, A.J. Christopher & Co, New York.

Stout, M. (2005) *The Sociopath Next Door*, Broadway Books, New York.

Tuckman, B. (1965) 'Developmental Sequence in Small Groups', *Psychological Bulletin*, vol. 63, pp. 384–399.

Waterman, J.A. and Rogers, J. (1996) *Introduction to the FIRO-B®*. Consulting Psychologists Press, Inc., Palo Alto.

Index